E. W. KENYON

Author

(1867-1948)

Twentyfirst Printing
978-1-57770-008-1

Copyright 2013

by

KENYON'S GOSPEL PUBLISHING SOCIETY

Printed in U.S.A.

TABLE OF CONTENTS

THE CASE STATED

Unanswered prayers stand between the individual and a faith life.

Some have lost faith altogether. Many have turned to philosophical and metaphysical cults because their prayer lives were failures.

If we should ask the individual what he believes to be his greatest difficulty in his Christian walk, I believe invariably his answer would be, "I haven't enough faith. I know it is not God's fault. I know the promises are there in the Word. I have simply failed to get faith. I have prayed for it; I have fasted for it; but I don't know how to get it."

This little conversation took place between a husband and wife over the breakfast table:

"No, I am not losing my confidence in the Bible, but it does seem to me that after the years we have attended church we should have gotten somewhere.

"Today in the office the question of faith came up and I found that I had none. That is, I didn't have any positive, clear-cut faith in the Word as I have in business.

"I have faith in the things that we manufacture. I know that they will do the things we advertise they will do.

"I don't know that God's Word will do the thing that it is advertised to do. I would like to know where the difficulty is.

"Down at the office, when we face a problem we solve it, but in our church we just cover it up. We ignore it. I have ignored it as long as I can. I must know!"

This is the reason for this book. We have written it to answer the faith problem for thinking men and women.

3

Chapter I

THE BASIS FOR FAITH

"THIS faith business has me whipped", said a young man the other day.

The pastor preached on it Sunday. He didn't tell me how to get faith, but he told me the necessity of it, told what it could do.

"He quoted those wonderful sentences from the lips of the Master, 'All things are possible to him that believeth.' 'If you have faith as a grain of mustard seed . . . '

"I have tried to get it. I have done everything that I knew or anyone else could tell me, but it seems to be so elusive. Can you tell me where the difficulty lies?"

I liked him. He was so frank, so genuine. The distress in his eyes challenged me.

I said to him, "Faith comes through the Word of God.

"You have faith in the man for whom you work; if he promises you a raise in your salary, you wouldn't question it.

"You have faith in the bank where you do business. If they told you that your account was overdrawn, you wouldn't question it.

"You know that you and your word are one. You are back of your word, back of every word that you promise.

"God and His Word are one. God is back of every Word that He promises. Not only is He back of it, but His throne is back of His Word.

"He said, 'I watch over my Word to perform it.'"

"He is a business man. He knows that His Word is the foundation of everything, so He stands back of it.

"Jesus said, 'Heaven and earth shall pass away, but my words shall never pass away.'

"This is the thing that gives faith... the integrity of this Word."

"Faith comes by hearing the Word, understanding it, by it becoming a part of us.

"I am going to say a hard thing. I am sure you will understand me. Lying and deceit and dishonesty are the badges of the world.

"We see it in international relationship between nations.

"They have their secret service men listening in everywhere, robbing each other of blueprints of warships, etc., until there is no chance of security anywhere.

"This is the reason for our unbelief. The air is pregnant with it. When we come up against the Word of God which cannot lie and cannot be challenged, somehow or other we are unprepared to accept it.

"Satan is a liar and he is the god of this world.

"Jesus came as a Revelation of Truth. He is the only one who ever made men become honest, when to tell the truth meant that they would be burned at the stake.

"Here we see the foundation of this Faith. You come to know Jesus through the word. He introduces you to the Father.

"Then you begin to act on the Word, to test it out, as it were.

"After a bit you will find that acting on what Jesus said, or the Father said, becomes as natural as acting on the word of the man for whom you are working."

He said after careful thought, "Thank you. I believe I have learned something I have never seen before."

One Foundation

There is but one foundation for Faith, the Living Word.

As we become one with the Word in our actions, then faith becomes an unconscious reality.

You never think of your Faith, you only think of the need and His ability to meet it.

If you wish faith to grow and become robust and strong, soak in the Word, feed on it, meditate on it, until you become one with it in the sense that you are one with your business.

Find out what you are in Christ, what your privileges are, what He thinks of you, what He says of you.

You will find all this in the Word.

Chapter II

WHAT FAITH IS

"**F**AITH is giving substance to things hoped for."

Faith is grasping the unrealities of hope and bringing them into the realm of reality.

Faith grows out of the Word of God.

It is the warranty deed that the thing for which you have fondly hoped is at last yours.

It is the "evidence of things not seen."

You hope for finances to meet that obligation; faith gives assurance that you will have the money when you need it.

You hope for physical strength to do the work that you know you must do.

Faith says, "God is the strength of my life, of whom shall I be afraid?"

Sense Knowledge has given to the church Mental Assent, which looks so much like faith that many people cannot see the difference.

Mental Assent is seeing it, admiring it, saying "it is true, but not in my case."

Mental Assent agrees that the Bible is a Revelation, that it came from God, and that every Word is true, and yet when the crisis comes it does not work. It simply recognizes the truthfulness of that wonderful Book, but it does not act upon it.

Hope says, "I will get it sometime."

Faith says, "I have it now."

Mental Assent says, "It is beautiful. I know I should have it. For some reason I don't get it. I cannot understand it."

Sense Knowledge faith says, "When I see it, when I feel it, I will know I have it."

Real faith in the Word says, "If God says it is true, it is. If He says that 'By His stripes I am healed', I am. If He says that God shall supply every need of mine, He will do it. If God says He is the strength of my life, He is. So I go about doing my work because He is what He says He is, and I am what He says I am."

"If He says that I am strong, I am.

"If He says that I am healed, I am.

"If He says that He cares for me, I know that He does.

"So quietly I rest on His Word, irrespective of evidences that would satisfy the Senses."

Real Faith is built on the Word.

It is untarnished by Sense Knowledge.

It is as unconscious of itself as is the faith of a little child in its mother.

The child never says, "Now Mother, I believe your word. I know that if I ask you for a piece of bread you will give it to me." If it said such things it would frighten the mother. She would wonder what had happened to her child.

We have built around faith a strange wordology that is like a barb-wire entanglement.

You hear men and women cry "Lord, I believe. Help thou mine unbelief."

You hear them pray for faith.

You hear men tell God that they know that what He says is true, that every Word He has spoken is true.

All that indicates the dominion of Sense

Knowledge over their spirits, that the Word has not yet gained the supremacy in their lives.

Faith is the result of the Word dwelling in us.

I don't mean the Word committed to memory.

I mean the Word lived, practiced, until it has become a part of ourselves.

We meditate in it. We think deeply in it. We feed upon it. The Word becomes a very part of ourselves; this word of Faith builds into us confidence and assurance.

Sense Knowledge will fight every step of the way to hold us in the realm of things seen, felt and heard, but we persistently drive ourselves into the Word until the Word is a part of our being, the Word is real.

Chapter III

KINDS OF FAITH

GAVE an address on the New Creation in which I stated, without giving any Scriptural proof, that the disciples were not Born Again until the day of Pentecost, that salvation came as the result of faith in Jesus as our Substitute.

After the meeting a man said to me, "Wasn't Martha saved? She believed in Jesus. Wasn't Peter's declaration one that brought salvation?"

What kind of faith did men have in Jesus before His Death and Resurrection?

John 20:9 "For as yet they knew not the Scripture, that He must rise again from the dead."

This is a part of the dramatic story connected with the Resurrection of the Lord Jesus.

We know that salvation is dependent upon our faith in Jesus as a Substitute, that He died for our sins, and that He arose for our Justification.

So Martha's faith in Jesus is described in John 11:27, "She saith unto him, Yea Lord: I have believed that thou art the Christ the Son of God, even He that cometh into the world."

She did not have faith in Jesus as the One who had died and risen as her personal Substitute and Savior.

She had faith in Him as God's Son, as the Messiah that had been promised.

Peter made another confession of Jesus which is recorded in Matthew 16:16.

And Simon Peter answered and said, "Thou art the Christ, the Son of the living God."

That was not a confession that Christ had died for his sins and had risen for his Justification, but simply a confession of His Messiahship and His being the Son of God.

There is still another type of confession in the Four Gospels that is striking.

John 6:30 "They said therefore unto him, What then doest thou for a sign, that we may see, and believe thee? what workest thou?"

Notice the expression "that we may see and believe."

Perhaps we should turn to John 20:25 and read Thomas' declaration. Jesus had appeared to the disciples after His Resurrection. Thomas was not present. They told him what had taken place.

He said, "Except I shall see in his hands the print of the nails, and put my finger into the print of the nails, and put my hand into his side, I will not believe."

He was willing to believe if He could have the evidence.

Jesus met him. 27-29 verses "Thomas, Reach hither thy finger, and see my hands; and reach hither thy hand, and put it into my side; and be not faithless, but believing. Thomas answered and said unto him, My Lord and my God. Jesus saith unto him, Because thou hast seen me, thou has believed: blessed are they that have not seen, and yet have believed."

Here are two kinds of faith in contrast.

One is Sense Knowledge Faith, which is based upon physical evidence. We see and believe. We hear and believe.

Jesus speaks of another kind of faith where they do not see, nor feel, nor hear, yet they believe.

11

The Faith that men had in Jesus during His earth walk was Sense Knowledge Faith.

This is one of the most startling discoveries we have ever made in this faith walk.

It clears up so many issues.

The great body of the church has Sense Knowledge Faith, rather than faith in the Revelation that God has given to us.

During the earth walk of Christ the Jews were under the First Covenant.

They were under the blood of bulls and goats.

They did not have Eternal Life until Christ died and rose again, for none of them believed in Christ as a Savior.

They did not believe in His Substitutionary work. They knew nothing of it.

Luke 24:10-53 gives a vivid picture of the condition of the disciples after the Resurrection of the Lord Jesus.

He had appeared to Mary and to the others.

They rushed to the place where the disciples were gathered.

"Now they were Mary Magdalene, and Joanna, and Mary the mother of James; and the other women with them told these things unto the apostles, And these words appeared in their sight as idle talk; and they disbelieved them."

There was no saving faith on the part of the disciples at that time.

They did not hail Him as their Savior.

They were mystified, staggered by His appearance.

They recognized Him for they saw the evidence

of the crucifixion in His body. They knew it was He.

The disciples had faith in Jesus as a Messiah, as the Son of God, but not as a Substitute, not as a Savior from sin. They saw Him as their Deliverer from Rome.

The knowledge of Christ's substitutionary work did not come to them clearly until God gave it to Paul.

We have it in His Revelation to Paul in the Epistles.

Faith, as Seen in the Book of Acts

Let us notice the faith that the disciples had as recorded in the first fifteen chapters of the book of Acts before the Pauline Revelation became known.

Acts 1, The disciples met the Master. They touched Him. They ate with Him. They heard his voice. Their faith in Him was based upon Sense Evidence.

It is not the kind of faith that you have. You have never seen Jesus physically. You have never heard His voice. You have never touched His body, yet you believe He arose from the dead.

They had lived with Him before His death.

They had lived with Him again for forty days after His Resurrection.

Read carefully Acts 2:1-4.

"And when the day of Pentecost was now come, they were all together in one place. And suddenly there came from heaven a sound as of the rushing of a mighty wind, and it filled all the house where they were sitting. And there appeared unto them tongues parting asunder, like as of fire; and it sat upon each one of them. And they were all filled with the Holy Spirit, and began to speak with other tongues, as the Spirit gave them utterance."

They heard the sound as of the rushing of a mighty wind.

They saw the tongues like as of fire parting asunder upon the brow of each one.

They heard them speak in tongues and glorify God.

There was no Revelation faith; it was purely Sense Knowledge Faith.

They believed in tongues because they heard them.

They believed the Spirit had come because they had seen the evidences.

The mighty miracles that followed, which are recorded in Acts, 5, gave the multitudes great faith in the Resurrection of the Lord Jesus.

It was not the kind of faith that you have today, because you have no such physical evidences as they had in Jerusalem.

I John 1:1-4 "That which was from the beginning, that which we have heard, that which we have seen with our eyes, that which we beheld, and our hands handled, concerning the Word of life (and the life was manifested, and we have seen, and bear witness, and declare unto you the life, the eternal life, which was with the Father, and was manifested unto us); that which we have seen and heard declare we unto you, that ye also may have fellowship with us; yea, and our fellowship is with the Father, and with his son Jesus Christ."

There were Peter and others who had seen Jesus with their own eyes after the Resurrection, and with their own hands they had handled Him.

Jesus had given them the right to use His Name and to lay hands upon the sick.

They manifested this authority.

Acts. 3:6 Peter and John used the Name to heal the impotent man at the beautiful gate of the temple.

The multitude could see the man whom they had known as a helpless cripple, healed before their eyes.

The Sanhedrin could say nothing when they arrested them.

Acts 4:14 "And seeing the man that was healed standing with them, they could say nothing against it." It closed their mouths.

Peter did not say on the day of Pentecost when they asked, "Men and brethren, what must we do to be saved," that they were to believe on the Lord Jesus Christ.

He simply said, "Repent, and be baptized everyone of you in the Name of Jesus Christ unto the remission of your sins."

The Revelation of faith had not yet come. God was dealing with them as children.

He did not ask them to believe anything they could not see, hear or feel.

It may be interesting to note that many times believers have said to us, "We want a primitive type of Christianity such as the church had in the first few years of its existence."

They did not know that by attempting to get that type of Christianity they were repudiating real faith, and the Word.

They declare that no one ever received the Holy Spirit unless he has received a physical manifestation.

They do not believe God is in the midst of people unless there is Sense evidence.

That is not faith in the Word of God. That is faith in the Senses.

I "saw it"; I "heard it"; I "felt it". Therefore, I believe that I have it.

15

Galations 3:2-3 "This only would I learn from you, Received ye the Spirit by the works of the law, or by the hearing of faith? Are ye so foolish? having begun in the Spirit, are ye now perfected in the flesh?" (Or senses).

You can see that God has dealt in great grace with us as children, when by reason of time we should have grown up and learned to walk by faith and not by sight.

If you will study carefully the first fifteen chapters of the book of Acts, you will notice there is not the slightest evidence that any of them understood the teaching of Substitution.

There is not one hint of the great teaching of Righteousness.

There is no indication they understood what the New Birth meant.

They enjoyed it; they walked in the fullness of it; but they did not understand it.

That was to come later through the Revelation the Father was to give to the Apostle Paul.

We would naturally expect that in the book of Acts there would be an opening of the great subjects: Redemption, Substitution, the New Creation, the ministry of Jesus at the right hand of the Father, but there is not an inkling of them.

The nearest of anything like that in the books is found in Acts. 15:10-11, at the council at Jerusalem.

Paul laid before the apostles the message he had preached.

Then Peter said, "Now therefore why make ye trial of God, that ye should put a yoke upon the neck of the disciples which neither our fathers nor we were able to bear? But we believe that we shall be saved through the grace of the Lord Jesus in like manner as they."

16

He had reference to the keeping of the law under the First Covenant. The last statement is in regard to the Gentile believers.

Before we take up Revelation faith, we should notice the different kinds of faith that men have in Jesus today.

Christian Science, Unity, and the other Metaphysical and philosophical teachers of today do not believe that God is a person.

They will tell you that He is a perfect mind, but He has no location.

It is just a great universal mind which finds its home in every individual. He has no headquarters.

It is a mind without a brain, without a personality.

They do not believe in sin as Paul taught it in the Revelation given to him.

They do not believe that Jesus died for our sins, but that He died as a martyr.

They do not believe He had a literal Resurrection, a physical Resurrection, but as one puts it, "a metaphysical resurrection." (whatever that means)

If God is not a person and Jesus did not put sin away, then who is Jesus and what is the value of our faith in Him?

One of them calls Him "The way-shower". He is not a way-shower. HE IS THE WAY!

Their faith in Jesus and their faith in God is, after all, faith in themselves and what they inherently have within themselves.

It has caused mighty changes in them, but it has never produced a New Creation, nor brought them into real fellowship with the Father God, nor given them Righteousness.

17

What is the faith that the modernists have today?

It is not faith in Jesus as a Substitute, for they do not believe in the Substitutionary Sacrifice of Christ.

It is not faith in God the Father as unveiled to us by Jesus.

It is faith in man's conception of Jesus. It does not produce a New Creation.

It does not save the lost.

Man has faith in science and loudly proclaims science as the modern god of the human.

But science is but the fragments of knowledge that man has gathered out of the great body of hidden truth in the universe.

He has gained this knowledge through the Five Senses.

These Five Senses have been unable to find the reason for Creation or the cause of Creation.

They have not discovered the source of Life or Motion, or the Authority or Power that holds the Universe together.

They do not know the Reason for man, nor the end of man. As Sense Knowledge is limited, so Sense Knowledge Faith is limited.

Chapter IV

THE DIFFERENT PHASES OF FAITH

AITH has never been given a "square deal" by the Church, yet it has given birth to all of man's greatest achievements.

Woolworth had faith in five and ten cent pieces and left behind him a fortune of $60,000,000 and stores at every crossroad.

Ford had faith in a low-priced automobile that every man could afford to buy.

Faith is the greatest element in advanced civilization.

As human faith gives birth to such achievements in the natural realm, so the believer's faith in the Father and His Word gives birth to spiritual achievements.

The preacher who has faith in the message that he is giving, finds that the Word produces faith results in the hearts of the men who hear him.

He has faith in the Word, that God is in it and back of it.

He has faith in humanity, that it will respond to the thing he is giving.

He has faith in Love, the Jesus kind of Love. He believes it is the solution of every human problem, and the family that practices love produces the highest type of Christian character.

It was a great day in my own life when I discovered that God was a Faith God.

I knew He was a Love God. I knew He was a Righteous God, an Omnipotent God, an Omniscient God; when I found He was primarily a Faith God I saw that it was natural for us, as His children, to walk by faith.

Creative Faith

Hebrews 11:3 "By faith we understand that the worlds have been framed by the Word of God, so that what is seen hath not been made out of things which appear."

It was a fresh, new creation . . . not a revamped creation made out of worn out worlds.

I discovered that it was ruled by Words. Heb. 1:3 "Who being the effulgence of his glory, and the very image of his substance, and upholding all things by the word of his power, when he had made purification of sins, sat down on the right hand of the Majesty on high."

There are three great words used again and again in the first chapter of Genesis. They are: "Let there be."

Faith-filled words brought the universe into being, and faith-filled words are ruling that universe today.

Jesus gave us some illustrations of creative faith.

Matthew 15:30-31 records that the maimed were made whole.

"And there came unto him great multitudes having with them the lame, blind, dumb, maimed and many others, and they cast them down at his feet; and he healed them; insomuch that the multitude wondered, when they saw the dumb speaking, the maimed whole, and the lame walking, and the blind seeing; and they glorified the God of Israel."

I have known of several women who have had organs restored that surgeons had removed through operations.

Creative faith is just as real today as it was when Jesus walked in Galilee.

Dominating Faith

This is faith that rules circumstances.

In Hebrews 1:3 we see a picture of Jesus.

"Who being the effulgence of his glory, and the very image of his substance, and upholding all things by the word of his power, when he had made purification of sins, sat down on the right hand of the Majesty on high."

Here He is not only a creator, but He also dominates what He has created.

He rules the universe by the Word of His power.

Here is an illustration of His dominating the forces of nature.

Matt. 8:26 "Then he arose and rebuked the winds and the sea; and there was a great calm."

Jesus ruled the wind and the sea.

How His authority staggered those who observed it.

They said, "What manner of man is this that commandeth the winds and the waves and they obey him?"

In Luke 5:1-11 we see Him ruling the fish of the sea.

He had used Peter's boat for a little while as a pulpit. Then He paid for the use of it.

He said, "Peter did you catch anything last night?"

Peter answered, "No, Master."

Jesus said, "Put out into the deep and let down your nets."

Peter said, "I know Master there are no fish here, but at thy word I will let down the nets."

The nets were filled instantly.

That is dominating faith.

Mark 1:32-34 "And at even, when the sun did set, they brought unto him all that were sick, and them that were possessed with demons. And all the city was gathered together at the door. And he healed many that were sick with divers diseases, and cast out many demons; and he suffered not the demons to speak, because they knew him."

Jesus ruled demons and they recognized His dominion over them.

John 11:39-44 At the raising of Lazarus He was Master over death.

He said, "Roll away the stone." Then He commanded Lazarus to come forth.

Jesus had dominating faith.

He ruled demoniacal forces. He ruled the works of the Devil. He was Master.

He commanded a tree to die and it died from the roots up.

He was absolute Monarch of the laws that govern the Universe.

Religious Faith

Few of us realize what a mighty force religious faith is today.

Men have faith in Creeds, in Organizations, in their Church, in Medicine, in Doctors, in Medical Science and Surgical Science, in good works, kindly deeds, giving money, in repentance and penance.

It is amazing the faith the average man has in something that he or someone else can do.

Faith in Experiences

Perhaps the most delusive of all the different kinds of faith is faith in Experiences.

Men tell what they have felt, what they have heard or seen.

Someone said to me recently, "I am not healed, I have not been able to demonstrate my faith."

Such people have Sense Knowledge Faith.

They must have physical evidence or they do not believe.

No delusion that has grasped the modern church is more deadly than this.

Some do not believe that they have received the Holy Spirit until they have had a physical manifestation.

They do not believe they are healed until the pain has left their body.

They do not believe God has heard their prayer until they can see some physical evidence of it.

We have seen in this type of faith that Sense Knowledge and Sense Evidence hold the place that the Word of God should hold.

In Revelation Faith the Word holds the first place. It is not dependent upon physical evidence. Revelation Faith believes that no Word from God is void of power, and rests in quiet confidence in what God has stated.

It accepts the Word as final without any other evidence.

If the Word declares it, that is enough.

The sick one reads, "Surely he hath borne my sicknesses and carried my diseases," and he cries, "Thank you, Father. Then I am healed."

This is New Covenant or Revelation Faith.

Chapter V

REVELATION FAITH

HERE are three great scriptures in the Old Testament on which the Pauline Revelation is based.

The first one is Gen. 15:6 "And Abraham believed God and He reckoned it unto him for righteousness."

This means that he had made an "unqualified committal" unto Jehovah and He reckoned it unto him for righteousness.

This "unqualified committal" is identical with the thought in Romans 10:9-10, "Because if thou shalt confess with thy mouth Jesus as Lord, and shalt believe in thy heart that God raised Him from the dead, thou shalt be saved; for with the heart man believeth unto Righteousness; and with the mouth confession is made unto salvation. For the scripture saith, Whosoever believeth on Him shall not be put to shame."

Revelation Faith as given to Paul demands a confession with our lips of the Lordship of Jesus. This means an "unqualified committal" to the Word, because the Word takes the place of the absent Christ.

The second Scripture, Isaiah 28:16, "Behold, I lay in Zion for a foundation a stone, a tried stone, a precious corner stone, a sure foundation; he that believeth shall not make haste."

There are two other translations: "Whosoever believeth on him shall not wander about distractedly seeking another foundation," or, "Whosoever believeth on Him shall not be put to shame."

It says that whosoever does this shall not be put to shame. Regardless of circumstances, of appearances, or sense evidences, he rests his case absolutely on the

Word.

The third Scripture is Habakkuk 2:4. "My righteous one shall live by faith." It carries us a step further.

"My righteous one" has been made Righteous by a New Creation. He is to walk, not by sight or by feeling, he is to walk by faith. In other words, he is to walk by the Word.

2 Cor. 5:7 "For we walk by faith, and not by sight."

Hebrews 10:38 "My Righteous one shall live by faith: And if he shrink back, my soul hath no pleasure in him."

You notice in each one of these scriptures a challenge for our confidence.

You are His Righteous one. You are to live by faith.

You are not to draw back to Sense evidences and to Sense Knowledge, but you are to walk on with Him in the light of the Word.

You will do as Abraham did.

You are looking at the Word and you wax strong through faith, giving glory to God, for you reckon that God is able to make good in you all that He has promised in His Word.

You can see how these great Scriptures become the foundation of the Revelation of Righteousness by faith in the Word as it is found in the Pauline Epistles.

You will find at the beginning of his great argument in the book of Romans that Paul uses Abraham's faith as a type.

Romans 4:3-5 "For what saith the scripture? And Abraham believed God, and it was reckoned unto him for righteousness. Now to him that worketh, the reward is not reckoned as of grace, but as of debt. But to him that worketh not, but believeth on him that justifieth the ungodly, his faith is reckoned for righteousness."

Righteousness means the ability to stand in God's presence without the sense of sin, guilt, or inferiority.

You will notice that after God reckoned Righteousness to Abraham that he made his great appeal for the salvation of Sodom and Gomorrah.

Read carefully Genesis 18 and see the fearless faith of Abraham.

He was not Righteous as we are Righteous. His Righteousness was merely reckoned to him.

It was set to his account. It gave him credit with God.

The Scripture we just read from Romans 4 tells us that Righteousness is not reckoned on the ground of works.

This Righteousness is granted on the ground of faith. One does not work for it. He accepts a gift.

Eph. 2:8-9 "For by grace have ye been saved through faith; and that not of yourselves, it is the gift of God; not of works, that no man should glory."

Salvation, Redemption, Eternal Life, the New Creation, the Indwelling presence of the Spirit, the legal right to use the Name of Jesus, and all of our privileges as sons and daughters of God, are based upon grace through faith.

No one earns them. No one has a better position than another.

Every person has the same Righteousness, the same privileges, the same standing, for it is all of grace.

Abraham's faith is described in Romans 4:18-21. "Who in hope believed against hope, to the end that he might become a father of many nations."

This is a startling statement. Faith had a combat with hope, and faith won.

Hope is always future. Faith is always now.

Hope would have robbed Abraham of a son, but faith combatted with hope, defeated it, and received as the reward, Isaac.

19th verse, "Without being weakened in faith he considered his own body now as good as dead (he being a hundred years old), and the deadness of Sarah's womb; yet, looking unto the promise of God, he wavered not through unbelief, but waxed strong through faith, giving glory to God, and being fully assured that what He had promised, He was able also to perform."

This is a beautiful picture of faith.

Abraham had nothing to rest upon except the Word of an angel.

Yet he believed that Word; he looked upon his own body and said to himself, "I am ninety- nine years old. I have passed the age where I can be the father of a child."

He thought of Sarah, ninety years of age. He knew that she was too old to bear a child.

Yet, turning away from the evidence of his Senses, he looked at the Word that God had spoken through the angel, and he waxed strong through faith, giving glory to God. For he said without doubt or fear, "God is able to make good what He has promised."

This is not Sense Knowledge faith. This is Revelation Faith. This is the kind of faith which Paul has given to us in his Revelation.

Notice the twenty-second verse: "Wherefore also

27

it was reckoned unto him for Righteousness."

He did not have the Righteousness we have. He had it set to his credit.

Romans 4:23-25 "Now it was not written for his sake alone, that it was reckoned unto him: but for our sake also, unto whom it shall be reckoned, who believe on Him that raised Jesus our Lord from the dead, who was delivered up for our trespasses, and was raised because we stand right with God." (Lit. Trans.)

The Pauline Revelation shows that God wrought a perfect Redemption in Christ.

Col. 1:13-14 "Who delivered us out of the authority of darkness, and translated us into the kingdom of the Son of His love; in whom we have our Redemption, the remission of our sins."

Eph 1:7 "In whom we have our Redemption through His blood, the remission of our trespasses, according to the riches of His grace."

Romans 3:26 "For the showing, I say, of His righteousness at this present season: that He might Himself be righteous, and the righteousness of him that hath faith in Jesus."

That Redemption was a redemption from Satan's dominion. It was a redemption from the guilt and penalty of sin.

It was a Redemption of our physical body from the dominion of disease.

It was a Revelation of a New Creation created in Christ Jesus.

That becomes a reality when we accept Christ as our Savior and confess Him as our Lord.

God gives to natural man His life and nature.

2 Cor. 5:17 "Wherefore if any man is in Christ, he

is a new creation: the old things are passed away; behold, they are become new. But all these things are of God, who reconciled us to Himself through Christ."

Eph. 4:23-24 "And put on the new man, that after God hath been created in righteousness and holiness of truth."

This Revelation of a New Creation is the most amazing fact of the grace of God.

God can take a Satan-ruled man, one who is called "sin" (because he is identified with Satan, he is a child of Satan), He can redeem him, take him out of this condition and impart to him His own nature, making him His own child.

I John 5:12-13 tells us what he has received.

"He that hath the Son hath the life; he that hath not the Son of God hath not the life. These things have I written unto you, that ye may know that ye have eternal life, even unto you that believe on the name of the Son of God."

John 6:47 "He that believeth hath Eternal Life."

A believer is a possessor. There is no believing without possession.

If I believe that God laid my sins upon Jesus and that Jesus was my Substitute, that He died in my stead, that He arose because He had put my sin away and had obtained Justification for me, the moment I believe I receive Eternal Life and become God's child.

Believing is having.

Next, He gives to us Righteousness. It is a Revelation of the Righteousness of God that becomes available to the man who has faith in Jesus. (Romans 3:21-26)

God becomes the Righteousness of the man who

takes Christ as his Savior and crowns Him as Lord of his life.

2 Cor. 5:21 "Him who knew no sin, He made to be sin on our behalf, that we might become the Righteousness of God in Him."

He not only becomes our Righteousness, but by the impartation of His nature we become His Righteousness, His sons and daughters.

Heb. 10:38 "My Righteous one shall live by faith."

We are called His Righteous ones.

Not only are we the Righteousness of God, but we have become the sons and daughters of God.

The climax of the Revelation that God gave to Paul, recorded in Romans 8:14-17 states this clearly.

"For as many as are led by the Spirit of God, these are the sons of God. For ye received not the spirit of bondage again unto fear; but ye received the spirit of adoption, whereby we cry, Abba, Father. The Spirit Himself beareth witness with our spirit, that we are the children of God: and if children, then heirs; heirs of God, and joint heirs with Christ."

This is sonship with all its glorious privileges.

Paul does not stop there. These sons and daughters are partakers not only of God's nature, but of God Himself in the person of the Holy Spirit.

Romans 8:11 "But if the Spirit of Him that raised up Jesus from the dead dwelleth in you, He that raised up Christ Jesus from the dead shall give life also to your mortal bodies through His Spirit that dwelleth in you."

I Cor. 6:19 "Know ye not that your bodies are the temples of the Holy Spirit which is in you?"

This all comes to the believer by faith.

There is no Sense Knowledge faith required.

You do not need to have any feelings to prove that you are Born Again.

All that is necessary is the Word of God.

Romans 10:9 declares: "Because if thou shalt confess with thy mouth Jesus as Lord, and shalt believe in thy heart that God raised Him from the dead, thou shalt be saved."

You do not need Sense Knowledge evidence to prove that you have received the Holy Spirit.

Luke 11:13 "How much more will your heavenly Father give the Holy Spirit to them that ask Him."

Your confidence is not in any physical manifestation or physical evidence. It is always in the simple Word of God.

Luke 1:37 "No Word from God is void of power" (or ability to make good).

These mighty Scriptures give one ground for Faith.

We have confidence when we know what we are in Christ.

Unbelief is largely the result of ignorance of what we are in Christ.

When I saw what God had done for me in Christ, my whole being was thrilled, faith was an unconscious fact, it was mine, He did it for me, I said "Thank you Father" and I began to enjoy my rights in Christ.

Chapter VI

SOME ENEMIES OF FAITH

HIS book would not be complete unless we revealed to you some of the beautiful enemies of faith.

The first one is "Hope".

Hope

Hope is always in the future.

"I hope that I will be healed."

"I hope that I will have money to meet my bills."

"I hope that I will have strength to do my work."

It is an enemy of faith. It stands in the way of faith.

I say to you, "Will you be healed when I pray for you?"

And you reply, "I hope so."

That means you will not be healed.

There is no healing in hope; as far as faith is concerned, hope is a delusion.

Faith is always present-tense. Therefore, because Hope is always future, it is a hindrance to Faith.

We have a hope of Heaven. When we reach Heaven we shall hope no longer

Mental Assent.

Mental Assent is another enemy, an adroit, dangerous enemy.

Mental Assent claims the whole Bible to be true. Mental Assentors say they believe every word of it, but they do not act upon it.

They simply assent to the fact that it is true.

I was called to pray for a woman with cancer. Both she and her husband had been outstanding Bible teachers for years.

As I sat by the bedside and opened the Word, she kept saying, "I have always believed that. I have known that Scripture since I was a child."

I went away from the house baffled, defeated. I could not understand where the difficulty lay.

When I arrived home, I walked up and down my room saying, "Lord, why is she not healed? She is a good woman. She says she believes your Word and has been a teacher of it for many years."

Then the Spirit made me see that she only mentally assented to the Word. She didn't believe it! Believing is acting on the Word. She had never acted on the Word for her healing.

A few days later I went to the house again. This time I understood her case.

As I began to open the Word she said, "I have believed that all my life." I told her, "No, you have never believed it, for if you had you would be out of bed doing your work. You only mentally assent to it."

Then I opened the Word again. She said, "That's the truth. I don't believe it. I can see now how I have never believed it. I have always assented to it."

You will find that in many cases where men and women have mental assent instead of faith, their creed or dogma has taken the place of the Word's reality.

Sense Knowledge Faith

Sense Knowledge faith requires Sense evidence.

This is the kind of faith Thomas had when he said,

(John 20:24-29) "Except I shall see in his hands the print of the nails, and put my finger into the print of the nails, and put my hand into his side, I will not believe."

Then Jesus suddenly appeared to him and said, "Reach hither thy finger, and see my hands; and reach hither thy hand, and put it into my side: and be not faithless, but believing. Thomas answered and said unto him, My Lord and my God. Jesus saith unto him, Because thou hast seen me, thou hast believed: blessed are they that have not seen, and yet have believed."

Here we see these two kinds of faith in contrast.

There is a Bible faith, and Sense Knowledge faith.

The faith that Mary and Martha and the others had in Jesus during His earth walk was Sense Knowledge faith. They believed in Jesus because they saw the miracles He performed.

The Jews said, "What doest thou for a sign that we may see and believe?"

This Sense Knowledge faith has almost driven real faith out of the churches.

This kind of faith does not give the Word its rightful place. Men carry the Word to Church, but they do not trust it. They trust in their feelings, in their emotions, in what they can see and hear, or taste, or smell.

Real faith is acting on the Word independently of any Sense evidence.

There are two kinds of unbelief.

The first is based on lack of knowledge. The man does not believe the Word because he knows nothing about it. So, he does not believe in the Father's Revelation to him.

A great number of unbelievers are ignorant of the things to believe. They do not know, so they cannot believe.

The second type of unbelief is mentioned in Heb. 4:11. It is "unpersuadableness."

"Let us therefore give diligence to enter into that rest, that no man fall after the same example of disobedience." (The Greek word is translated "unbelief" in the King James version. It is "disobedience" in the Am. Rev and means "unpersuadableness.")

This means that the man is unwilling to allow the Word to govern him.

It is a refusal to act on knowledge.

He knows what the Word teaches, but he refuses to act on it.

Believing is an act of the will.

He can act on the Word if he will.

"Believing" is "willing" to do His will.

Disobedience is an unpersuadable attitude toward the Word.

Then unbelief is either ignorance of the Word or unpersuadableness to act upon it.

Chapter VII

FAITH IN YOUR FAITH

AITH in your own faith is the law of success in the realm of the spirit.

You live in the Word and the Word lives in you.

The Word is a living thing.

When you let it loose in you, it is letting God loose in you.

When you dare to act the Word and speak the Word, God will be in the words that you speak.

As the Word gains the ascendancy, there will be an unconscious faith in your own ability to trust Him. You will trust Him utterly, you will go the limit of His Word.

It is a beautiful thing when a man abandons himself to the Word, swings utterly free, and lets God loose in him until "Greater is he that is in you than he that is in the world" becomes a thrilling reality.

1 Cor. 2:12 tells us that we have received the Spirit, that we may know the things that have been freely given to us of God.

"But we received, not the spirit of the world, but the spirit which is from God; that we might know the things that were freely given to us of God."

Get to know your place, your rights, your privileges, and your authority.

There will be no problem about faith then.

Faith is a problem only when we do not know the Lord and we do not know the Word.

Give place to the God inside of you.

Reckon on the God inside of you.

In the morning before you arise say, "I can do that because He is inside of me. He will enable me to meet these people. He will enable me to speak the Word. He will enable me to walk in love because, greater is love within me than jealousy and hatred around me."

Just reckon on the God inside of you.

Plan your work with the consciousness of His ability in you to put it over.

He has become a living reality.

He is in there now.

He awaits your demands upon Him.

He unveils Himself as your need demands it.

You are expecting Him to guide you into all truth or reality.

Whenever you take up the Word for a few minutes, you know that the light inside of you will open the Word and make it a living thing.

You know John 16:13 is absolutely true.

"Howbeit when he, the Spirit of truth, is come He shall guide you into all the truth."

He will take the Father's things and unveil them to you.

You have unconscious confidence in the Name when spoken through your lips.

You know that if you say, "In the Name of Jesus, demon come out of that man or woman" that he will come out.

You know when you command that disease to stop being that it will stop being.

You know when you take the Name of Jesus Christ for finances to meet an obligation that as sure as the

Father sits on His throne the money will come.

You know His Word in your lips will save the lost, heal the sick, give courage and strength to the weak and victory to the defeated.

Once it was God's Word in Jesus' lips.

Now it is God's Word in your lips.

Jesus believed in God's Word in His lips.

Your confidence in that Word makes it a living thing in your lips.

How rich and beautiful life becomes when the Word gains the ascendancy in our hearts!

It will be a great day to you when you know that your Faith does things, when you believe in your own ability to reach the ear of Love.

When you know that your prayers are answered, that God hears you, you are no longer dependent on another's Faith, you have your own.

Say it over and over again, "At last I have faith in my own faith. I can reach God as well as anyone else."

If a loved one is stricken, you fearlessly take your rights and deliver them from the enemy, your prayer prevails, your faith wins.

You can use the Name of Jesus as well as anyone now.

That Name is yours at last, with its "all authority" and you dare use it as your own. He gave you the right to use it, and you are doing it.

Knowledge is of no value unless you know how to use it.

You know your standing with the Father, you know your privileges, now act your part.

Faith in Other's Faith

The largest percentage of those who are healed in mass meetings, where they have mass faith, seldom ever maintain their healing.

The reason is obvious. They have no personal faith. It is just faith in other people's faith.

During our last trip to Los Angeles, a Christian worker who has been greatly used of the Lord said to me, "I cannot understand why my prayers for some of my old friends are not heard. They used to be healed every time I prayed for them."

I said, "The difficulty lies in the fact that when by reason of time those sick people ought to be praying for the sick themselves, they need someone else to pray for them."

Just as the Spirit says in Hebrews 5:12, "For when by reason of time ye ought to be teachers, ye have need again that some one teach you the rudiments of the first principles of the oracles of God; and are become such as have need of milk, and not of solid food. For everyone that partaketh of milk is without experience in the Word of righteousness; for he is a babe."

Everyone that partaketh of milk; that is, lives in the realm of the Senses and is dependent upon Sense evidence instead of the Word, has had no experience in the Word of Righteousness. He is still a babe.

What does it mean?

Those people who have been healed by someone else's faith for years, have reached a place where God demands that they have faith of their own.

If they are unwilling to study the Word, unwilling to develop their faith life, they will turn to the "arm of flesh" and suffer the penalty that naturally follows.

39

God expects every one of us to have experience in the Word of Righteousness. In other words, that we have experience of our own in praying for sick folks, in proclaiming the Word, in leading men to Christ, in unveiling the Word.

That belongs to every believer.

Colossians 1:12 "Giving thanks unto the Father, who made us meet to be partakers of the inheritance of the saints in light."

Here is a better translation, "Giving thanks unto the Father, who has given us the ability to enjoy our share of the inheritance of the saints in light."

He has delivered you out of the authority of darkness.

He has recreated your spirit.

Now He is ready to renew your mind so that you may understand your privileges and rights in Christ.

It belongs to you. You have a right to it.

You should enjoy it instead of being dependent upon someone else's faith.

You have a faith of your own now.

What an hour it would be if those who read this book should declare, "By the grace of God, I will have my own faith."

You have a right to it. It belongs to you.

You have the same Holy Spirit that I have, the same Holy Spirit that Jesus had, and that the Apostles had.

You have the same Eternal Life, the same Righteousness, the same ability.

The Father has no favorites.

All these things belong to every one of us, so we need not be barren or unfruitful.

2 Cor. 9:8 "And God is able to make all grace abound unto you; that ye, having always all sufficiency in everything may abound unto every good work."

And in the tenth verse he says, "And he that supplieth seed to the sower and bread for food, shall supply and multiply your seed for sowing, and increase the fruits of your righteousness."

You have the Righteousness that is imparted to you in the Nature of the Father at the New Birth.

That Righteousness should be bearing fruit in your daily life.

You should take advantage of the fact of your legal standing before the Throne, of your rights in Christ and begin to pray for the sick and needy.

You have the same Legal standing before God that Paul had and you have the same Righteousness that he had, there is no excuse to hide your light beneath a bushel.

Begin to witness of what you are in Christ.

Chapter VIII

CORRESPONDING ACTIONS

EYMOUTH gives us a striking expresssion in James 2:14 "What good is it my brethren, if a man professes to have faith, and yet his actions do not correspond?"

18th verse, "You notice that his faith was cooperating with his actions, and that by his actions his faith was perfected."

One of the gravest mistakes that many believers make is to confess their faith in the Word, and at the same time contradict their confession by wrong actions.

A woman said to me, "I cannot understand why I did not get my healing. I have prayed and prayed. I know the Bible is true."

I asked her, "Are you still taking medicine?"

"Oh, yes," she said.

Then I read her this scripture that I have just quoted. Her actions did not correspond with her confession. She said she was trusting the Lord and yet her trust was in medicine and not in His Word.

We say we trust the Father for our finances, and at the same time we are worrying and fretting how we are going to pay our bills.

One minute we confess that no Word from God can ever be forfeited, that He must keep His Word with us, and that we know that He will, and the next moment we are repudiating all that we have confessed.

James tells us there must be corresponding action.

"Be ye doers of the Word, and not hearers only deluding your own selves."

The actions of a "doer of the Word" coincide with his confession.

Jesus said, Matt. 7:24-26 "Therefore whosoever heareth these sayings of mine, and doeth them, I will liken him unto a wise man, which built his house upon a rock: and the rain descended, and the floods came, and the winds blew, and beat upon that house; and it fell not: for it was founded upon a rock.

"And every one that heareth these sayings of mine, and doeth them not, shall be likened unto a foolish man, which built his house upon the sand: and the rain descended, and the floods came, and the winds blew, and beat upon that house; and it fell: and great was the fall of it."

So many who profess Christ and who declare they believe the Word from Genesis to Revelation, and they say it with a great deal of unction are not doers of the Word. They are talkers about the Word. They have mentally assented to the fact that the Word is true.

It does them no good. They are not making it their own.

When I trust in the Word with all my heart, and stop leaning upon Sense reason, stop looking to people for deliverance, then there are corresponding actions.

My actions are in perfect fellowship with my confession.

It has taken some of us a long time to have corresponding action with our confession.

Until there is corresponding action, there will be continual failing.

I may confess as loudly as I please that God is the strength of my life and at the same time tell about my weakness, my inability, and my lack of faith.

There is no corresponding action here.

I am resorting to human means rather than trusting in the Lord utterly.

That is bound to bring confusion in my spirit and weakness and failure in my life.

Let us turn resolutely to I Peter 5:7 "Casting all your anxiety upon Him for He careth for you."

Regardless of circumstances, regardless of influences about us, let us turn every problem into His care.

Your worst enemy is yourself. It has come through Sense Knowledge that would limit you to your own ability.

The language of the Senses is: "I can't, I haven't the ability, I haven't the strength, I don't have the opportunity, I have no education, I have been limited."

The language of faith says, "I can do all things in Him who strengtheneth me."

Who is it that strengthens me? It is my Father God.

I can do all things through Him. I cannot be conquered. I cannot be defeated.

There isn't force enough in all the world to conquer Him who dwells in me.

Not only am I born of God, a partaker of God's nature and life, but I have God dwelling in me, and I have the Spirit of Him who raised Jesus from the dead dwelling in me.

I have God's wisdom, God's strength, God's ability.

I am learning how to let Him govern my intellect, letting Him think through me, use my vocal faculties. I am daring to think His thoughts after Him.

I am daring to believe that it is God who is at work within me and that He will work His own good pleasure.

I am daring to say in the presence of my old enemies: failure, weakness, want, lack of opportunity, lack of knowledge, lack of strong friends, and a thousand others, "God is my ability."

God has made me greater than my enemies.

God has made me put my heel on the neck of weakness, of fear, of inability, and I stand and declare that whosoever believeth in Him shall not be put to shame.

I cannot be put to shame.

My weaknesses are routed.

The strength of God is mine.

The ability of God has taken me captive and I revel in this captivity.

That is Faith speaking, real corresponding action.

Chapter IX

WITH THE HEART MAN BELIEVETH

OR years I have been eagerly searching for a satisfactory explanation of Romans 10:10. "With the heart man believeth unto righteousness."

You understand that the word "heart" is used illustratively because the heart is the life center of man. It is the great pumping station that keeps the physical body alive.

We have come to know that when God speaks of the heart, He means the human spirit.

We know that man is a spirit.

He is in the same class as God.

We know that God is a spirit and that He became a man and took on a man's body, and when He did it He was no less God than He was before He took the physical body.

We know that man, at death, leaves his physical body and is no less man than he was when he had his physical body.

We know that man cannot know God through Sense Knowledge.

God is only revealed to man through the spirit.

It is the spirit of man that contacts God.

We know that spiritual things are just as real as material things.

God is just as real a person as though He had a physical body.

Jesus, with His physical body now in Heaven, is no more real than the Holy Spirit or the Father.

I Peter 3:4, our spirit is called the "hidden man of the heart."

In Romans 7:22 it is called "the inward man".

This "inward man" and "the hidden man" give us Gods definition of the human spirit.

The real man is spirit.

He has a body and a soul.

The soul contacts the intellectual realm, the physical body contacts the physical realm, and the spirit, the spiritual realm.

That explains how "the natural man understandeth not the things of the spirit of God for they are foolishness unto him, neither can he know them because they are spiritually understood." I Cor. 2:14.

The first two chapters of I Cor. give us a contrast between Sense Knowledge and spiritual knowledge, or between the senses and the spirit.

You understand that all the knowledge that man has outside of Revelation Knowledge has come to him through these five doors to the mind.

They are the means of communication between material things and intellectual.

The mind can receive nothing unless it receives it through these Five Senses. (The subject is covered more fully in our book "The Two Kinds of Knowledge").

If The Five Senses were destroyed, man would have no means of receiving knowledge.

He could not know himself, nor the material world.

2 Cor. 4:16 "Wherefore we faint not, but though our outward man is decaying, yet our inward man is being renewed day by day."

Eph. 3:16 "That He would grant you according to the riches of His glory, that ye may be made strong with His ability through His Spirit in the inward man."

When a man is Born Again, Eternal Life is imparted to his spirit, to this inward man.

When the Holy Spirit comes into his body, He comes in to dwell in his spirit.

The Holy Spirit cannot communicate directly with our minds, but He must communicate with us through our spirit which reaches and influences our intellectual processes.

The spirit has a voice. We call that voice conscience, or a hunch, or guidance.

Sometimes it is called intuition. We get a hunch and if we follow it we do not make a mistake. (I do not like the word "hunch" but it is in common use).

We all know that if we had followed an inward voice, we would never have made some of the investments that we have made where we lost money; that we would never have chosen certain people as companions; we would never have gone into business with certain people.

That inward voice seeks to give guidance to our minds.

We would almost never make a mistake if we would learn to give heed to our spirit.

One of the greatest mistakes that has been made in our intellectual culture has been the ignoring of the spirit.

Knowledge of our intellects has taken the throne, and our spirits have been locked away in a prison.

Consequently we are continually making mistakes because our spirit which should guide us is not permitted to function.

Knowledge is something that we acquire through the Senses, through reading, through travel and hearing.

Wisdom is the ability to use the knowledge to profit.

Wisdom does not come through the Senses.

Wisdom comes from our spirit.

James says that it comes down from above. That is divine wisdom, God's wisdom imparted to us. James 3:13-18.

The man who shuts his spirit away and makes a prisoner of it, who never listens to it, never obeys it, becomes crippled and is an easy prey to selfish and designing people.

The one who lets the spirit gain the mastery and influence him at crisis times is the one who climbs to the top.

What does it mean to "believe with the heart"?

It means to believe with the spirit.

We cannot believe with our intellect. That goes without argument.

Faith is a product of the spirit.

This inward conviction, this thing called assurance, is a child of our spirits.

We don't know why we know; we cannot explain it, and yet we do know.

The other day I was unfolding the Word to a woman who had a very painful sickness. As I opened the Scripture step by step she said, "I see it, By his stripes I am healed."

I said, "How do you know you are healed?" She said, "Because the Word declares that I am."

Sense Knowledge said, "The sore is still in your body and you can feel the pain even now."

Yet she arose above Sense Knowledge and Sense Evidences and declared that she was healed.

As I prayed for her, her faith absolutely drove out the disease. The thing that meant death to her was gone. Why? Because in her heart she believed the Word of God; in her spirit she believed it.

How does our spirit get faith that our intellect cannot obtain—through the Word.

Jesus said, "Man shall not live by bread alone, but by every Word that proceedeth out of the mouth of God." Matt. 4:4.

He is speaking of spiritual food. He is using Sense Knowledge terms to convey a spiritual truth.

Our spirits become filled with assurance as we meditate in the Word.

For many years I have walked by faith for our finances, for all my physical needs. Now I have grown to see that the Word is the food that builds the spirit, makes it strong, and gives to it its quiet assurance.

The Senses believe in what they can hear and see and feel.

The spirit believes in the Word, regardless of seeing, hearing, or feeling.

The people who are prayed for again and again but do not get their healing, have Sense Knowledge faith.

They do not have Revelation faith. They have faith in man, faith in the anointing oil, faith in someone else's prayer, faith in some person or organization. They do not have faith in the Word.

James 5:14 illustrates this: "Is any sick among you?

50

Let him call for the elders of the church; and let them pray over him, anointing him with oil in the name of the Lord. And the prayer of faith shall save the sick, and the Lord shall raise him up." Then it tells how the prayer of a Righteous man availeth much in its working.

This whole picture is a Sense Knowledge faith picture.

If the one who was sick had known that "by His stripes" he was healed, he would have had no need to call for the elders.

But because he did not know it, in his desperation he turned to the Lord and to the elders.

Here is a demonstration of the Grace of God, in meeting man on his own level as Jesus did in the Incarnation.

When the Word was made flesh and dwelt among men, He came into man's Sense-Knowledge realm, so that man could see Him, hear Him, touch Him.

Everything connected with the earth walk of Jesus as far as man could see, was in the Sense realm.

There was no faith in Jesus from a spiritual point of view.

They believed because they saw the miracles and ate the bread.

When He died on the cross there was no spiritual apprehension. They did not know that He was dying for their sins. They thought He was dying as a martyr for His ideals.

Sense Knowledge holds the same conception today.

The scholastic world believes Jesus died for His convictions.

51

At the Crucifixion Sense Knowledge-faith broke down.

To believe with all our hearts is to believe independently of Sense Knowledge.

Our Spirits respond to our yielding to the Lordship of Jesus. (The key to Biblical faith is the recognition of the Lordship of Jesus by the heart.)

I Peter 3:15 "But sanctify in your heart Christ as Lord."

"Sanctify" means to "separate" or "set apart". We set Christ apart in our hearts.

When we crown Jesus as Lord of our lives, we crown His Word as Lord of our lives. This gives the Word its proper place.

Jesus is seated at the right hand of the Father. His Word is in our hearts.

We give to that Word its place, and when we do faith becomes perfectly natural.

Prov. 3:5-7 "Trust in the Lord with all thy heart, and lean not unto thine own understanding (or to Sense Knowledge). In all thy ways acknowledge Him and He will direct thy paths. Be not wise in thine own conceit."

Be not wise with Sense Knowledge which leads us to repudiate the Word or to act independently of it.

2 Cor. 10:3 "Casting down reasonings and every high thing that exalts itself against the knowledge of the Word of God, and bringing every thought into captivity to the obedience of Christ."

This is very important if we want to walk by faith. The Word must be superior to Sense Knowledge, whether that Sense Knowledge be ours or someone else's.

We want to remember that Sense Knowledge is

always limited.

No man has perfect Sense Knowledge.

The Word of God is perfect. This Revelation is His perfect Revelation and it meets every crisis and every need of our lives.

If we trust this Word with all our hearts then there comes a quietness and rest into our spirits.

Believing is knowing. We know that the Word of God is true.

When He says, "And my God shall supply every need of yours," we simply know in our spirits that every need will be supplied and we don't worry; we have no anxiety.

Our hearts take courage as we read the Word. Our assurance becomes deeper.

This is assurance which is independent of Sense evidence. It may contradict Sense evidence as it often does, but we know that spiritual things are as real as material things.

We know that spiritual things are superior to physical things, for God, a spirit, created physical things.

We know that spiritual forces are stronger than physical forces.

We know that "Greater is He that is in us than he that is in the world."

We know that the Greater One is master of disease and weakness.

We trust in Him with all our hearts; He rises up in us and gives our minds illumination which they can get from no other source.

We know we cannot be conquered.

We know because we believe.

Chapter X

ACTING ON HIS WORD

 N John 6:47 Jesus said, "He that believeth hath eternal life."

"Believing" is "having". It is possession.

Mental Assent admires the Word, confesses that the Word is true and very desirable, but it doesn't possess.

Believing ends in the glad confession, "It is mine. I have it."

How little real action on the Word we see today.

You remember the man who was brought into the presence of Jesus by four of his friends. (Mark 2:1-12)

Jesus said to him, "rise, take up thy bed and walk."

Had he not acted on the Master's words, he never would have been healed; but because he acted, he was healed.

Luke 5:5 Peter said, "But at thy word I will let down the net."

What a change would come into some of our lives if we said, "At Thy Word I will."

We have clung to the theories of men and ignored the Living Word.

Healing and victory belong to you.

When Jesus said to Peter, "Come, walk the waves with me", Peter acted on the Word.

When the servants filled the firkins with water, they obeyed what Jesus said, and the water became wine. John 2:1-11.

We mentally Assent to the integrity and the reality

of the Word; but we do not act on it.

Until we act upon it, it does not become a reality.

You may hold the Resurrection Truth as a great doctrine or dogma, but it will not mean anything to you until you say, "He died for me. He conquered death and hell for me. He arose for me. And because He arose I am a victor, I am a conqueror of Satan today. Satan has no dominion over me. I am free." Then the Word becomes something more than a doctrine or a theory. It becomes a reality.

People who act on the Word receive things.

Today, the one who acts on the Word receives.

You act faith, you talk faith; your actions and your words agree.

You are a believer.

It took faith to get into the family, but after you get into the family all things are yours. (1 Cor. 3:21)

It took faith to become a child of God, but the children own all that Christ wrought for them.

When God says, "I watch over my Word to perform it", then you may be certain that if you accept Isaiah 53:3-6 that just as surely as God sits on His throne, healing is bound to be yours.

All you need to do is act on the Word.

It is deeply important that you learn this simple little lesson.

It is not struggling, or praying, or crying.

It is acting on what God has spoken that brings results.

Faith and Believing

The word "faith" is a noun: the word "believe" is a verb.

"Believing" is really "acting" on the Word.

It is simply acting on the Word of God as you have acted on the word of a physician, the word of a lawyer, or the word of a loved one.

You don't ask the questions: "Do I believe?" or "Have I faith?"

You simply say, "That is what God has said," and you act accordingly; or "Did God say that 'by His stripes' I am healed? If God said it, then I must be healed, and I will act on what God has spoken."

Faith is the result of action.

Believing is taking the step up to the object, the thing you want. Faith is having arrived.

Instead of using the word "believe", I use the words "act on His Word."

It is simpler. It is perfectly Scriptural and it is just what Jesus meant.

It is a remarkable thing that nowhere in the Epistles did Paul urge believers to believe or have faith.

Our urging men to believe is a result of the Word's having lost its reality.

What does Paul tell us?

Eph. 1:3 "Blessed be the God and Father of our Lord Jesus Christ, who hath blessed us with every spiritual blessing in the heavenlies in Christ."

If He has blessed you with every spiritual blessing, then you are blessed.

You don't need to ask for the spiritual blessings.

All you need to do is thank Him that you have them.

All you have to say is, "Father I thank Thee for my healing. I thank Thee for my deliverance."

All that Jesus did was to act upon His Father's Word.

56

All that Peter did was to act upon the Word which Christ had given him.

It was the Word of Christ in Peter's mouth that he acted upon that brought salvation and healing and deliverance to the people.

We may preach the Word, but if we do not practice it, it will produce no results.

We may preach healing and declare our faith in healing, but that is of no value unless we practice it.

James tells us that "faith without corresponding actions is dead."

When we act on the Word we show our faith.

We know that no Word from God is void of power or void of God's ability. Luke 1:37.

So, we act on it. We fearlessly lay our hands on the sick. We command the disease to leave in Jesus' Name and it obeys. The sick one is healed.

He said, "I watch over my Word to perform it."

We would never have laid hands on the sick and claimed healing if He had not told us to do it.

He said, "They that believe shall lay hands on the sick." Mark 16:16-18.

That means the instant we accept Christ as our Savior, confess Him as Lord, and receive Eternal Life, we can begin to function in the Family. We can begin to lay hands on the sick.

"He that believeth and is baptized shall be saved." Mark 16:16.

The Greek word there for "saved" is "sozo" which means "healed."

Healing in the final analysis is spiritual as well as physical.

Disease manifests itself in the physical, but its roots, its substance, its reality are in the spirit.

The word "believe" occurs about one hundred times in the Gospel of John.

The word "faith" only occurs about two or three times.

The reason evidently is that he was talking to men outside of the Body of Christ, to Jews under the Law.

They were not men of faith. They did not have faith. He was inciting them to believe.

Some Facts About Believing

Some people cannot believe the Word because they have never confessed the Lordship of Christ.

The fear of man has held them in bondage.

This is one of Satan's strongest holds on man.

Many times a dead creed imprisons a man.

You have been taught not to believe this and not to believe that.

Your Christ has been lost in a maze of theological theories.

Abandon yourself to the Lordship of the Word; act on it, and God will become real to you.

Chapter XI

THINGS THAT BELONG TO US

HE Father in His great grace has given to the Church enough to make it rich and strong.

Eph. 1:3 "Blessed be the God and Father of our Lord Jesus Christ who has blessed us with every spiritual blessing in the heavenlies in Christ."

What does He mean by this?

In His redemptive work all that God did in Christ from the time He was made Sin until He sat down at the right hand of the Majesty on High, belongs to the Church, the Body of Christ.

We have been blessed.

Jesus did nothing for Himself and the Father needed nothing.

John 3:16 "For God so loved the world that He gave His only begotten Son, that whosoever believeth on Him should not perish, but have eternal life."

Jesus was the Father's gift to a lost world.

He has never taken back the gift.

The world owns Jesus, whether or not it acknowledges the ownership.

All that Jesus did in His Substitutionary Sacrifice is the private property of the individual for whom Jesus did it.

The sinner does not need to beg God to save him.

The work has already been accomplished.

All that he needs to do is to accept it and thank God for it. Then it becomes his.

"For by grace have ye been saved through faith; and that not of yourselves, it is the gift of God; not of works, that no man should glory." Eph. 2:8-9.

Salvation is a gift.

Faith comes by acting on the Word of God.

We act on the Word. We take Jesus Christ as our Saviour, confess Him as our Lord, and we receive Eternal Life that very moment.

"For we are His workmanship created in Christ Jesus."

The work was accomplished before Christ arose from the dead, and that work belongs to us now.

All we need to do is to accept it.

The believer does not need to ask the Father to heal him when he is sick, because "Surely he hath borne our sickness and carried our diseases; yet we did esteem him stricken, smitten of God and afflicted."

God laid our diseases on Jesus.

Isaiah 53:10 states that it pleased Jehovah to make Him sick with our sicknesses so that by His stripes we are healed.

If we are healed then we do not need to pray for our healing.

All we need to do is to rebuke the enemy in Jesus' Name, order him to leave our bodies, and thank the Father for perfect healing.

It is all so simple.

We do not need to pray for the Lord to give us strength, because He is now the strength of our lives.

Psalm 27:1 "Jehovah is my light and my salvation; Whom shall I fear? Jehovah is the strength of my life: Of whom shall I be afraid?"

This belongs to us now.

He has become our light and our salvation. That is, He has become our knowledge and our redemption.

He has become our deliverance.

1 Cor. 1:30 "But of him are ye in Christ, who was made unto us wisdom from God, and righteousness and sanctification, and redemption."

Let us look at the things that God made Jesus become to us.

We don't ask to be sanctified, because He is our sanctification.

We don't ask to be made Righteous, because He is our Righteousness and we became His Righteousness in Christ.

A believer is a possessor.

"He that believeth hath eternal life."

We cannot believe without having Eternal Life.

We cannot believe Philippians 4:19 "And my God shall supply every need of yours" without being possessors of the things we need.

Paul recognized that believers were possessors.

We don't have to try to believe that we are redeemed because we are redeemed. Eph. 1:7.

We don't have to try to believe that we are in Christ because we are in Him. 2 Cor. 5:17.

We don't have to try to believe that we are the sons of God because we have been re-created. We are in His family. I John 3:2.

We don't have to try to believe that He will remit our sins, and pray to that end, because our sins are remitted and we stand acquitted, justified in His presence. Our old sin nature has been put away and we have received the nature of God. Col. 1:13-14.

We don't have to try to believe that God will give us the Holy Spirit.

All we need to do is invite Him to come in. "How much more will your heavenly Father give the Holy Spirit to them that ask Him." Luke 11:13.

He is talking to a new babe in Christ who has never received the Spirit.

He is speaking to one who has received Eternal Life. Now he definitely asks the Spirit, who raised Jesus from the dead, to come into his body and make His home there.

The Name of Jesus belongs to us.

God is our own Father.

Jesus is our own Lord, Advocate, and Master.

The Holy Spirit is our Teacher.

Healing is absolutely ours. Strength is ours. Light and wisdom are ours.

Eternal Life belongs to us.

He is our supply. He is our sufficiency. He is love in us.

All this is ours when we first believe and is not dependent on our individual faith now as a believer.

We possess it. We own it. It belongs to every child.

All is in Redemption.

Just thank the Father, praise Him whenever a need confronts you that is covered by Redemption, and it is yours.

Some may say, "What then can we pray for?"

We can pray for a great needy world, Christians who live in darkness beneath their privileges, deliverance for men and women from bondage from which they do not know they have been freed.

Enjoying Our Rights in Christ

Redemption was God planned; its results satisfy the heart of God and meet every need of man.

Christianity links us with God. If we are in union with God we are successful.

The mightiest forces of the universe are at our disposal.

The ability of God is our heritage.

Acts. 1:8 "Ye shall receive ability when the Holy Spirit is come upon you." (The King James version of this scripture reads "power" instead of "ability".)

God's ability is at our disposal.

What a thrilling fact it is.

I John 4:4 "Ye are of God my little children and have overcome them, because Greater is He that is in you than he that is in the world."

We are of God.

Our roots sink down into God.

God's ability is our inheritance. Just as the roots draw the moisture out of the soil, so our roots in God draw the strength and vitality and ability of God.

He is not only with us, but He becomes a part of us.

He is in us. His nature is ours.

It would help us to say over and over again during the day "God is in me. God's ability is mine. God's strength is mine. God's health is mine. His success is mine. I am a winner. I am a conqueror. I am a success because the Greater One, with His great ability is in me."

It is not our giving up, but it is our taking on.

It is our enjoying this Life with Him. It is our living with Him, fellowshipping, laboring with the Man of the Ages.

We have the use of His Name, the Name that conquers, the Name that is above every name.

The Name of Jesus can be used in the business world, in the scientific world. It can be used in every department of human endeavor.

"In my Name." It is actually as though the Master Himself were here.

"Whatsoever ye demand in my Name I will do it."

When we use that Name, we bring Jesus Christ into actual contact with our problems.

The source of all power is linked up with our lives and the problems that confront us.

Chapter XII

HINDRANCES TO FAITH

AITH never rises above its confession. (We do not refer to the confession of sin, but the confession of the Word.)

If we confess weakness and failure and sickness, we destroy faith.

When we boldly make our confession that our diseases were laid on Jesus and we hold fast to that confession, we bring God on the scene.

Sometimes lack of knowledge will hinder us from making a bold confession.

We do not act on the Word beyond our knowledge.

Faith grows with understanding of the Word.

Lack of knowledge of our Redemption and of our redemptive rights is oftimes the reason for unbelief.

Lack of Understanding

Lack of understanding of what the New Creation means and what it actually is, hinders our faith life.

Many people do not know that they have Eternal Life. They think of themselves as being "saved from sin".

Many people are not God-Inside-Minded.

Lack of understanding of their place in Christ and of Christ's place in their lives, lack of understanding of Righteousness, what it is and what it gives, holds more people in bondage than perhaps anything else.

When we know that we are the Righteousness of God in Christ, we step out of the narrow place of failure and weakness in which we have lived, into the boundless fullness of God.

Lack of understanding of our legal right to the use of the Name of Jesus holds us in bondage and gives us a sense of weakness. But when we know what the Name will do, we can defeat Satan and enjoy victory.

Many are failures because of a lack of understanding about confession.

Our faith keeps pace with our confession.

We are held in bondage because we lack understanding about acting on the Word.

We try to believe.

All that is necessary is for us to act on what God says.

If we know that Word is true, we act as though it were true and it becomes a reality in our lives.

Real faith is the child of knowledge of the Word.

The Two Confessions

Our faith is measured by our confessions.

Our usefulness in the Lord's work is measured by our confessions.

Sooner or later we become what we confess.

There is the confession of our heart, and the confession of our lips.

When the confession of our lips perfectly harmonizes with the confession of our hearts, and these two confessions confirm God's Word, then we become mighty in our prayer life.

Many people have a negative confession.

They are always telling what they are not, telling of their weakness, of their failings, of their lack of money, their lack of ability, and their lack of health.

Invariably they go to the level of their confession.

A spiritual law that few of us have recognized is that our confessions rule us.

When we confess His Lordship and our hearts fully agree, then we turn our lives over into His care.

That is the end of worry, the end of fear, the beginning of faith.

When we believe that He arose from the dead for us, and that by His Resurrection He conquered the Adversary and put him to nought for us, when this becomes the confession of our lips and our hearts, we become a power for God.

If we have accepted Him as our Savior and confessed Him as our Lord, we are New Creations; we have Eternal Life; we have the position of sons; we are heirs of God and joint heirs with Jesus Christ.

The moment that we recognize the fact of His actual Resurrection, then we know that the sin problem is settled; we know that Satan has been eternally defeated for us.

We know that we are in union with Deity.

We know that we have come into the family of God.

We know that the ability of God has become ours.

This may not dawn on us all at once, but as we study the Word and act upon it, live in it, and let it live in us, it becomes slowly perhaps, but surely a living reality.

That reality is developed through our confession.

We confess His Lordship and we declare before the world that He is our shepherd and that we do not want.

We confess that He makes us to lie down in green pastures, and that He leads us beside the waters of stillness.

We confess that He has restored our souls to a sweet, wonderful fellowship with Himself.

We confess that He has made us New Creations, that old things have passed away and behold all things have become new, and that we have become the Righteousness of God in Christ.

We confess fearlessly before the world our utter oneness and union with Him.

We declare that He is the Vine and we are the branches; that the branches and the Vine are one.

We declare that we are partakers of the Divine Nature that dwelt in Him as He walked in Galilee.

These are our confessions.

We have come to know that Satan is defeated, that demons are subject to the Name of Jesus in our lips, that disease cannot exist in the presence of the Living Christ in us.

Now we dare to act on what we know the Word teaches.

We dare to take our place and confess before the world that what the Word says about us is true.

We are done with the confession of failure, of weakness, of inability, because God has become our ability, God has become our sufficiency and He has made us sufficient as ministers of a New Covenant.

We confess that He has taken us out of the old realm where failure reigned, into the new realm of victory, joy, and peace.

As we make our confession and act on the Word, our faith grows and our Redemption becomes a reality.

The Right Confession

Jesus said, "For I spake not from myself; but the Father that sent me, he hath given me a commandment, what I should speak." John 12:49.

Every healing that Jesus performed was wrought through His Father's Word. Every Word that He spoke was the Father's Word.

Jesus knew who He was; He knew His place; He knew His work.

He was always positive in His message. He knew the words that He spoke were His Father's Words.

He took His place as a son. He acted His part.

He continually confessed His sonship.

Jesus always confessed what He was.

He said, "I am the Good Shepherd. I am the Bread of Life. I am the Water of Life. God is My Father. I am the Light of the World."

In John 5:19-30 Jesus makes ten statements about Himself.

They are really confessions, and every one of them links Him up with Deity.

He was speaking His Father's own Word.

John 7:29 "I know Him; because I am from Him, and He sent me."

He not only confessed what He was, but He also fearlessly confessed what man would be after he became a New Creation.

John 15:5 "I am the vine, ye are the branches."

John 7:38-39 "He that believeth on me, as the scripture hath said, from within him shall flow rivers of living water. But this spake he of the Spirit, which they that believed on him were to receive: for the Spirit was not yet given; because Jesus was not yet glorified."

What a confession that was and how real it became on the Day of Pentecost!

John 8:54 "If I glorify myself, my glory is nothing: it is my Father that glorifieth me; of whom ye say, that he is your God; and ye have not known him: but I know Him; and if I should say, I know him not, I shall be like unto you, a liar: but I know him, and keep his word."

John 17:5 "And now Father, glorify thou me with thine own self with the glory which I had with thee before the world was."

That was a remarkable testimony.

John 17:26 "And I made known unto them thy name, and will make it known."

Jesus knew the new name that God was to receive.

John 17:6 "I manifested thy name unto the men whom thou gavest me out of the world."

I have a conviction that the new name which Jesus speaks of here is "Father."

No one had ever called Him "Father" before.

John 9:35-36 "Jesus heard that they had cast him out; and finding him, he said, Dost thou believe on the Son of God? He answered and said, And who is he, Lord, that I may believe on him?"

Jesus then confessed who He really was.

In the 37th verse, Jesus said to the man who had been blind, "Thou hast both seen him, and he it is that speaketh with thee."

Jesus openly declared that He was the Son of God.

In John 4:26 we have another startling confession.

He was talking with the woman of Samaria and

He confessed that He was the Messiah, the Son of God.

Jesus Knew Who He Was

Nearly every miracle that Jesus performed was performed with the Father's Words in Jesus' lips.

Jesus was the revealed will of the Father.

John 4:34 "My meat is to do the will of him that sent me, and to accomplish his Work."

John 5:30 "I seek not mine own will, but the will of him that sent me."

John 6:38 "I am come down from heaven, not to do mine own will, but the will of him that sent me."

John 8:29 "For I do always the things that are pleasing to him."

What a picture of the Master! He had no personal ambitions, no personal ends to achieve. He was simply doing the will of His Father, unveiling the Father until He could say, "He that hath seen me hath seen the Father." (John 14:9)

The less worldly ambitions we have, the less worldly desires, the more fully the Father will unveil Himself to us.

His Words in our lips will perform the same prodigies that His Words performed in Jesus' lips.

Self-seeking limits one.

The selfish man is a limited man.

He who lives in the Word and lets the Word live in him, he who practices the Word and acts upon it, is the one who reveals the Father.

When we act upon the Word of God we unveil the Father.

The Wrong Confession

Few of us realize that our confession imprisons us. The right kind of confession will set us free.

It is not only our thinking; it is our words, our conversation, that builds power or weakness into us.

Our words are the coins in the Kingdom of Faith. Our words snare us and hold us in captivity, or they set us free and become powerful in the lives of others.

It is what we confess with our lips that really dominates our inner being.

We unconsciously confess what we believe.

If we talk sickness, it is because we believe in sickness. If we talk weakness and failure, it is because we believe in weakness and failure.

It is surprising what faith people have in wrong things.

They firmly believe in cancer, ulcers of the stomach, tuberculosis, and other incurable diseases. Their faith in that disease rises to the point where it utterly dominates them, rules them. They become its absolute slaves.

They get the habit of confessing their weakness and their confession adds to the strength of their weakness. They confess their lack of faith and they are filled with doubts.

They confess their fear and they become more fearful. They confess their fear of disease and the disease grows under the confession.

They confess their lack and they build up a sense of lack which gains the supremacy in their lives.

When we realize that we will never rise above our confession, we are getting to the place where God can really begin to use us.

You confess that by His stripes you are healed; hold fast to your confession and no disease can stand before you.

Whether we realize it or not, we are sowing words just as Jesus said in Luke 8:11 "The seed is the word of God." The sower went forth to sow and the seed he was sowing was the Word of God.

That is the seed we should sow. Others are sowing Sense Knowledge seeds of fear and doubt.

It is when we confess the Word of God, declare with emphasis that "By His stripes I am healed" or "My God supplies every need of mine" and hold fast to our confession that we see our deliverance.

Our words beget faith or doubt in others.

Rev. 12:11 declares "And they overcame him because of the blood of the Lamb, and because of the word of their testimony."

They overcame him with the Word of God that was in their testimony. They conquered the Devil with words.

Most of the sick that Jesus healed during His ministry were healed with words.

God created the Universe with words: faithfilled words.

Jesus said, "Thy faith has made thee whole."

He said to dead Lazarus, "Come forth." His words raised the dead.

Satan is overcome by words, he is whipped by words.

Our lips become the means of transportation of God's deliverance from heaven to man's need here on earth.

We use God's Word. We whisper, "In Jesus' Name demon come out of him."

Jesus said, "In my Name ye shall cast out demons, in my Name ye shall lay hands on the sick and they shall recover."

All with words!

I question whether the hands do more than register to the Senses. It is the Word that heals.

Jesus said, "Whatsoever ye demand in my Name, that will I do." (In the Greek the word "ask" is "demand.")

We are demanding just as Peter did at the Beautiful Gate when he said, "In the Name of Jesus Christ of Nazareth, walk."

Words healed that man.

Now we make our confession of words. We hold fast to our confession. We refuse to be defeated in our confession.

John 8:32 "And ye shall know the truth, and the truth shall make you free."

Or John 8:36 "If therefore the Son shall make you free, ye shall be free indeed."

We know that the Son has set us free and we confess it.

Jesus is the High Priest of our confession.

Christ conquered the enemies of humanity: Satan, sin, sickness, fear, death and want.

He made them captives and He set man free.

Heb. 4:14 tells us to hold fast to the confession of our faith.

"Having then a great high priest, who hath passed through the heavens, Jesus the Son of God, let us hold fast our confession."

That confession is faith speaking. It is our victory over the enemy. It is our confidence.

Col. 2:5 in one of our translations reads "For although, as you say, I am absent from you in body, yet in spirit am I present with you and am delighted to witness your good discipline and the solid front presented by your faith in Christ."

That "solid front" means continual confession of victory.

We never confess anything but victory.

Romans 8:37 "Nay, in all these things we are more than conquerors through him that loved us. "

Jesus disarmed the principalities and powers which fought against Him and put them to an open shame. This is Col. 2:15 from Connybeare's Translation.)

We should stop making the wrong kind of confession, and begin at once to learn HOW to confess and WHAT to confess.

We should begin to confess that we are what He says we are, and hold fast to that confession in the face of every contrary evidence.

We refuse to be weak or to acknowledge weakness.

We refuse to have anything to do with a wrong confession.

We are what He says we are.

We hold fast to that confession with a fearless consciousness that God's Word can never fail.

Chapter XIII

PRAYER

RAYER is joining forces with the Father. It is a fellowship with Him, carrying out His will upon the earth.

It seems that God is limited by our prayer life, that He can do nothing for humanity unless someone asks Him to do it.

Why this is, I do not know.

We get a hint of it in Gen. 18 when God refused to destroy Sodom and Gomorrah until He had talked it over with His Blood Covenant friend, Abraham.

Prayer Under the Old Covenant

Abraham's prayer, which is recorded in Gen. 18:22-23, is the most illuminating and suggestive of any prayer in the Old Covenant.

He said to God, "Wilt thou consume the righteous with the wicked? Peradventure there are fifty righteous within the city: wilt thou consume and not spare the place for the fifty righteous that are therein? That be far from thee to do after this manner, to slay the righteous with the wicked; that be far from thee: shall not the Judge of all the earth do right?"

Here Abraham was taking his place in the Covenant.

Abraham had through the Covenant received rights and privileges that we little understand.

The Covenant that Abraham had just solemnized with Jehovah gave him a legal standing with God.

We hear him speak so plainly, "Shall not the Judge of all the earth do right?" This is his intercession for

Sodom and Gomorrah.

All through the Old Covenant we find men who understood and took their place in the Covenant.

Joshua could open the Jordan. He could command the sun, moon and stars to stand still in the heavens.

Elijah could bring fire out of heaven to consume the offering as well as the altar.

David's mighty men were utterly shielded from death in their wars. They became supermen as long as they remembered the Covenant.

Practically all the prayers of the Old Testament were prayers of Covenant men.

They had to be answered. God had to give heed to their petitions.

Prayer Under the New Covenant

The New Testament is a New Covenant.

The believer has Covenant rights in prayer.

Isaiah 43:25-26 "I, even I, am He that blotteth out thy transgressions for mine own sake; and I will not remember thy sins. Put me in remembrance; let us plead together: set thou forth thy cause, that thou mayest be Justified."

Here is a challenge of the Covenant-keeping God to Israel.

It is a challenge to the church.

"Put me in remembrance." In other words remind Him of His promises in regard to prayer.

Men who have been mighty in prayer have always reminded God of His promises and laid the case legally before Him.

When you pray, stand before the throne and plead your case as a lawyer.

That lawyer is continually bringing law and precedent.

Bring His Word, His Covenant promises, plead your rights.

"Put me in remembrance. Set forth thy cause that thou mayest be Justified."

It is the challenge of God to lay the case before Him.

If your children are unsaved, find a scripture that covers your case and lay the matter before Him.

Isaiah 45:11 "Ask me of the things that are to come; concerning my sons, and concerning the work of my hands, command ye me."

This is prophetic. It does not apply to Israel. It is yours.

"Ask me of the things that are to come." These were future things, things perhaps connected with your life and your family, your community or your government.

"Concerning the work of my hands, command ye me."

This is in perfect harmony with John 15:7 "If ye abide in me, and my words abide in you, ask whatsoever ye will, and it shall be done unto you."

The word "ask" means "demand".

You do not command in tones of arrogance, but as a partner.

You lay the case before Him.

You call His attention to His part in the drama of life.

A scripture you should use continually is Isaiah 55:11.

Read carefully the 9th and 10th verses: "For as the

heavens are higher than the earth, so are my ways higher than your ways, and my thoughts than your thoughts."

"For as the rain cometh down and the snow from heaven, and returneth not thither, but watereth the earth, and maketh it bring forth and bud, and giveth seed to the sower and bread to the eater; so shall my Word be that goeth forth out of my mouth: it shall not return unto me void, but it shall accomplish that which I please, and it shall prosper in the thing whereto I sent it."

This is the very backbone of the prayer life.

No Word that has gone forth from God can return unto Him void.

Jer. 1:12 "I watch over my Word to perform it."

He will make good His Word, if you dare stand by it.

Jehovah's Remembrancers

Isaiah 62:6 "Ye that are Jehovah's remembrancers, take ye no rest, and give Him no rest, till He establish, and till He make Jesusalem a praise in the earth."

Here He suggests there are men and women who are "remembrancers", whose business it is to hold these promises and these statements of fact clearly before the Lord's mind.

Isaiah 64:7 "And there is none that calleth upon thy name, that stirreth up himself to take hold of thee; for thou hast hid thy face from us, and hast consumed us by means of our iniquities."

Daniel stirred himself up to pray. He gave himself to prayer.

He called God's attention to the promises He had made through Jeremiah. There would be a restoration of Israel. They should go back again to the promised

79

land. Their captivity in Babylon should end.

Read carefully Daniel 9.

Satan tries to oppose prayer and stand in the way of it.

Read the story of the combat of angels and demons over Daniel recorded in Dan. 10:20.

Jer. 33:3 "Call unto me, and I will answer thee, and will show thee great things, and difficult, which thou knowest not."

God is challenging our cooperation with Him in the prayer life. He wants to bless us.

Psalm 78:41 (marginal rendering) "And they turned again and tempted God, and limited the Holy One of Israel."

We have done that.

We have limited Him with our prayer life.

We have let the great promises of fellowship and cooperation with God go by as untouched, unrealized.

Jesus was not only a teacher of prayer, but He was a prayer.

I wish there had been a record given us of the things for which He prayed and the method of His prayer.

We know that He left the multitudes again and again, to spend sometimes a whole night with His Father in prayer

Whether that was purely for fellowship, or whether He was praying for a lost world, we cannot tell.

United Prayer

Matt. 18:18-20 gives us a picture of united prayer.

"What things soever ye shall bind on earth shall be bound in heaven; and what things soever ye shall loose on earth shall be loosed in heaven. Again I say unto you, that if two of you shall agree on earth as touching anything that they shall ask, it shall be done for them of my Father who is in heaven. For where two or three are gathered together in my name, there am I in the midst of them."

This scripture is amazing. "Where two or three are gathered together in my Name, there am I."

That would be an executive meeting with the Master.

We come together to do business, sitting in His presence, planning, discussing and then praying, for He said, "If two of you shall agree."

The group may be very small, just a husband and wife, but if they agree as touching anything they shall ask, it shall become. This is a challenge.

Every believer should find an agreer, someone who could join with him in prayer.

We should lay out a program of prayer, making a list of subjects and of people to lay intelligently before the Father.

John 15:7-8 "If ye abide in me, and my words abide in you, ask whatsoever ye will, and it shall be done unto you. Herein is my Father glorified, that ye bear much fruit; so shall ye be my disciples."

If we are Born Again, we do abide in Him.

His Word abides in us in the measure that it governs our lives, in the measure that we act upon it.

The problem of faith does not enter prayer.

It is supposed that those who abide in Him have faith.

It took faith to get into the family.

We are in the family now, and it is not a problem of faith.

It is a problem of the Word abiding in us.

If we are living the Word, then when we come to pray, that Word dwells in us so richly it will become His Word on our lips.

It will be as the Father's Words on the Master lips.

How to Pray

John 15:16 "Ye did not choose me, but I chose you, and appointed you, that ye should go and bear fruit, and that your fruit should abide; that whatsoever ye shall ask of the Father in my name, He may give it you."

Prayer here is addressed to the Father in Jesus' Name. This is divine order.

This statement has enwrapped within it the ability to bring God into our circumstances, into our finances or whatever the need may be in our homes, in our business, or in our nation.

"Whatsoever ye shall ask of the Father in my Name, He will give it you."

We are not praying to Jesus. We are praying to the Father in the Name of Jesus.

Jesus really gives us the power of attorney. That means that what Jesus can do, we can do.

That means that Jesus' Name gives us the right to go into His presence and see our prayers answered.

Jesus backs our prayer. He makes it good.

John 16:23-24 "In that day ye shall ask me nothing. Verily, verily, I say unto you, if ye shall ask anything of the Father, He will give it you in my name. Hitherto ye have asked nothing in my name: ask, and ye shall receive, that your joy may be made full."

We are to pray to the Father in Jesus' Name.

We can fellowship and talk things over with the Master, but when it comes to prayer based on legal grounds, then it is directed to the Father, in Jesus' Name.

Nothing is impossible here.

We will not ask anything of the Father that is out of His will if we are walking with Him.

The word "faith" does not occur in this connection.

We had faith to come into the family; now everything that Jesus did belongs to us.

We are taking advantage of it.

We are acting the part of a child of God.

I John 5:14-15 "And this is the boldness which we have toward Him, that, if we ask anything according to His will, He heareth us: and if we know that He heareth us whatsoever we ask, we know that we have the petitions which we have asked of Him."

It Is The Father's Will

The believer, walking in fellowship with the Word, will never ask for anything outside of the Father's will.

We need not worry about that.

We know that saving the lost is in His will, for to this end Jesus died.

John 3:16 "For God so loved the world, that He gave His only begotten Son, that whosoever believeth on Him should not perish, but have eternal life."

We know that healing the sick is in His will, for Christ bore our infirmities and carried our pains.

I Peter 2:24 "Who His own self bare our sins in His body upon the tree, that we, having died unto sins, might live unto righteousness; by whose stripes ye were healed."

We know praying for finances to meet obligations is His will.

Phil. 4:19 "And my God shall supply every need of yours."

Practically everything is covered in these points.

We can pray for the ministers that they will speak; in the power of the Spirit.

We can pray for the lost in heathen lands.

All this is in His will.

With what boldness we should come to Him.

Matt. 19:26 "But with God all things are possible."

We are coming to Him who has all ability.

Speaking to the Jews He said in Matt. 21:22 "And all things, whatsoever ye shall ask in prayer, believing, ye shall receive."

Mark 11:24 "Therefore I say unto you, all things whatsoever ye pray and ask for, believe that ye receive them and ye shall have them."

Here is faith thanking Him for a thing that he already possesses which has not yet materialized, but he knows that it is his.

Mark 9:23 "All things are possible to him that believeth."

All things are possible to the man who cooperates with the Lord, who fellowships with the Lord, who is a co-laborer with the Lord.

Chapter XIV

SOME THINGS WE SHOULD BELIEVE

CHRISTIANS were called "believers" in the early church.

When Jesus said, "all things are possible to him that believeth" the Greek word used there for "believeth" means "a believing one."

He said, "These signs shall accompany them that believe," this word also means a believing one.

The believer really means a possessor, one who has accepted Christ, received Eternal Life, has taken his place in the family.

The professing Christian who is only a mental assenter lacks the reality of Eternal Life in his spirit. He hopes and yearns for it, dreams that some day he will have it, but the believer joyfully thanks the Father for it.

The word, believe, is a verb. The word, faith, is a noun. Everywhere Jesus uses the word, believe, he means possession.

John 6:47 "Verily, verily, I say unto you, He that believeth hath eternal life."

Believing there is equivalent to possession.

The same thing is true today.

Some Things Not To Believe

We should never believe in failure. We should never think or talk failure because we are believers.

The believer, in the mind of the Father, is a success.

He is God's own child.

We should never talk about lack or inability to do things.

We should never mention weakness.

We remember that God is the strength of our lives and that we have received God's ability.

Jesus said to the disciples that they were to tarry in Jerusalem until they received power from on high.

The Greek word translated "power" means "ability."

Then they were to tarry in Jerusalem until they received the ability of God.

We have never majored this. We have never heard it explained. How it grips our hearts. We hardly dare say it out loud: "God is my ability."

We have ability to do anything that the Master would have done.

We have ability to love the unlovely and the hateful just as He loves them.

Christ died for the ungodly and the unworthy.

We have the ability to live for these unworthy ones and these ungodly ones.

We have the ability to know the Word, because God is our ability. He is the author of the Word.

We should never talk hatred, because hatred is the badge of the adversary.

We should never allow ourselves to think it.

We should never for a moment permit ourselves to admit that wrong can win or that sin can conquer.

We are God's representatives. We are taking Jesus' place, doing Jesus' work.

We have His Name with all authority. We have Him as our wisdom.

We have Him as our ability.

If we only knew it, we are supermen.

If we could understand how He looks upon us, how He thinks of us, we would never again talk weakness and failure and lack.

We are in God's class of being. We are partakers of His nature.

We are taking the place of Jesus in His absence.

We are doing the kind of work that Jesus did.

"Greater things than these shall ye do, because I go unto the Father." Whatsoever ye shall demand in my name, that will I do that the Father may be glorified in the Son."

We step out of the old realm of the Senses where weakness and failure dominated into this new realm of success and victory.

We know that that Righteousness gives us access to the throne room of God and we have as much a right to go into the throne room as Jesus.

This puts prayer on a new basis. We are not pleading and crying, but we are going in as sons and daughters assuming our responsibilities and laying the needs of the world before Him.

Prayer becomes like an executive meeting.

We have come in to get a requisition to meet some special need.

Chapter XV

RECEIVING, NOT GIVING

WE have given a wrong message to the world. Our message to the world has been one of "giving and putting away;" we have told them what they must do, while the truth is that God does not ask the world to give up anything.

Someone might ask, "Doesn't He ask them to give up their sins?" Never.

"Doesn't He ask them to give up their wickedness and rebelliousness toward Him?" No.

It is not subtraction. It is addition.

It is not taking from, it is adding to.

God is the giver. We are the receivers.

"God so loved that He gave His only begotten Son." (Jn. 3:16)

He never asked humanity to give anything.

He saw our poverty. He saw that the only things we could give would be things for which He had no use.

God is the Giver.

He gives only as a prince, a king, can give.

He does not ask us to give up anything, or to give away anything.

He does ask us to receive something.

The first thing He offers is Redemption from the fear of want, failure, weakness, of sickness or disease. He gives us a Redemption from all these.

It does not seem credible or even possible that it could be and yet it is true.

He offers us a Redemption from the works of the enemy.

How it thrills the heart to contemplate it!

Col. 1:13-14 gives us the amazing truth "Who delivered us out of the authority of darkness and translated us into the kingdom of the son of His love."

Let us notice carefully. He does not ask us for anything.

He has come of His own accord, at His own expense, and Redeemed us out of the authority of darkness, weakness, ignorance and failure, and He sends the Revelation to tell us the good news that we are Redeemed; not that we may be delivered, not if we will be good and give up our sins. No . We are already delivered out of the authority of darkness.

In that word "darkness" is the entire system of bondage, of Satanic hatred, bitterness and jealousy.

Everything that Satan is, is in that word "darkness."

There is ignorance. There are tears. There is hunger. There is want. There is lack. There is sickness, pain and agony.

We are delivered out of it.

Who delivered us out of the authority of Satan's dominion.

He has not only delivered us but He has translated us into the kingdom of the son of His love in whom we have our Redemption, the remission of our trespasses.

How it grips our hearts.

This is not the message that they have taught us to preach.

This is the reverse of it.

Nowhere does He tell us to go out and club the sinner, tell him what he must give up, what he must surrender.

If he takes Christ as a Savior, that is repentance. If he confesses Him as his own Lord with his heart, that is believing.

He not only asks us to receive this marvelous Redemption, but He asks us to receive Jesus as Lord.

This is like Ruth, the Moabite, receiving Boaz as her husband. The receiving of Boaz meant the end of poverty and want, the end of biting anxiety and fear, the end of hunger and suffering.

She became the mistress of that mansion on the hill. Those great olive orchards and the pomegranate, the peach and the orange, those great fields of wheat became her own.

She did not give up her poverty. She received his wealth.

She did not give up her loneliness; she received his fellowship.

She did not give up her weakness and anxiety and fear; she received his plenty, his protection, his care.

God comes to us. He asks us to receive Jesus as our Lord and joyfully tell the world that we have reached the end of weakness and failure, that we have found His strength, His fulness, His ability.

The word "Lord" has the significance of the bread provider.

He is our bread provider. He is our strength provider.

He is our ability provider.

"Of His fulness have we all received and grace upon grace."

We are receivers.

We are no longer beggars crying that He come and bless us.

We are blessed with every spiritual blessing in the heavenlies.

We are rich with His riches.

We are full with His fullness.

We are satisfied with Him.

He is our risen Lord, our own.

He asks us to receive Eternal Life, His nature.

This makes us New Creations. We are created in Christ Jesus.

The old things of failure and weakness and sin are passed away and behold all things have become new. All these things are of God who has reconciled us unto Himself.

We did not reconcile ourselves. We had nothing to do with the reconciliation. We had nothing to do with the New Creation except to receive it.

It Is All Of God

We cannot grasp it. It is beyond us.

It is in the realm of the spirit, the realm of the riches of grace, of glory.

This New Creation makes us children of God Almighty.

God is now our Father. We are His children, we are in His family.

The wonder of it! The grace of it! The joy of it!

How it comforts and strengthens.

As we receive His Redemption we are free from

the old bondage and habits. As we receive His Lordship and joyfully tell it to the world, we receive our Redemption.

Eternal Life links us up with Him.

We didn't even ask Him for it.

We didn't plead and pray and promise we would do certain things if He gave it to us.

All we had to do was to acknowledge the gift, and thank Him for it.

"But," you say, "what about our sins?"

He put our sin away by the sacrifice of Himself.

We had nothing to do with it whatever.

We had been helplessly in bondage for years, and then one day someone came along and said, "Did you know He put your sin away by the sacrifice of Himself?"

We said, "Yes, we read it, but we never understood it."

The thing that bound us to the Adversary and the thing that brought condemnation had been put away, our hearts were filled with joy.

"He bore our sins in his body on the tree."

He was made sin with our sin that we might become Righteous with His Righteousness.

Sin no longer has any dominion over us.

"All we like sheep had gone astray. We had turned everyone to his own way" and the Father laid upon Christ all that we had ever been or done.

John the Baptist said, "Behold the lamb of God that beareth away the sin of the world."

God has dealt with the sin problem.

He does not ask us to deal with it. He does not ask us to do one thing with it. He does not even ask us to be sorry that we were sinners.

Why? We were not to blame for being sinners.

Is a man to blame for being born in a certain country? No. He had nothing to do with it.

We had nothing to do with our sin condition.

We could not even help committing the sins we committed. They were an outgrowth of a condition of sin in our nature.

Now He comes and tells us that He put that sin away, that He remitted all the sins we ever committed.

He is not asking us to do anything.

All Is Of Grace

He said, "By Grace are ye saved through faith, and that not of yourselves, it is a gift of God, and not of works lest any man should boast. For we are His workmanship created in Christ Jesus for good works." Eph. 2:8-10.

When was the New Creation a fact in the mind of the Father? When Jesus arose from the dead.

When were we justified and declared Righteous? When He arose from the dead and sat down at the right hand of the Majesty on high.

Then this New Creation, and Justification, and Righteousness has been waiting for us all these years? That is the fact.

He does not ask us to do anything but just receive it.

If we have to pay Him for our Redemption it is no longer of grace but of works.

"By grace are ye saved on the ground of faith and

it is not of works lest any man should boast."

Sonship is a gift.

Redemption is a gift.

Eternal Life is a gift. The New Creation is a gift. The Holy Spirit is a gift.

Jesus was a gift.

God so loved that He gave His Son.

Jesus is a gift, the Father's gift.

We do not pay for a gift.

Chapter XVI

THE SENSE-RULED MIND
(Romans 12:1-2)

OW few of us have realized that the Sense-Ruled mind can never have victorious Revelation Faith.

Only when the mind has been renewed through practicing the Word does faith in the Word become powerful.

This renewing of the mind comes by acting on the Word in every crisis, day by day, letting the Word have its place in the life.

The believer does not enjoy the Living Word until his mind has been renewed.

The unrenewed mind would rather feed upon the words of man. It cannot act upon the Word of God as it acts on the words of men.

People will tell you what the Doctor has said, and they will act on his word.

I tell them what God has said and they shake their heads and say, "No, we cannot act on that."

The Sense-Ruled mind is always waging war against unbelief.

It lives in the realm of fear and uncertainty. The Word is not final, it settles no issues; over and over again it has the same battle, only to lose.

It is because the Senses, rather than the Word, rule the mind.

The Sense-Ruled mind lives in a realm of uncertainty.

Until the Word gains mastery over it, it will be

swayed by feelings and by the things it sees and hears, rather than by this Revelation Knowledge.

When the Sense-Ruled people read the Word, they declare it to be true, but in the next breath they speak of Sense-Knowledge relief.

The sick one will declare that the Word is absolutely true, then turn from it to remedies.

The Sense-ruled mind does not settle down on the Word and rest quietly.

It has a double mind.

It says God's Word is true and is willing to argue about the absolute integrity of the Word, yet it is continually repudiating it in daily conduct.

James calls these people the double-minded folk who talk "faith" and act "reason."

They seek "faith" results from "reason" actions.

The double-minded are always unstable.

They live on the border land between faith and reason.

Their house is builded on the land between these two countries.

They seek to claim citizenship under both governments.

Faith cannot be builded except upon the Word of God.

Chapter XVII

THE NEW COMMANDMENT
AND RIGHTEOUSNESS

HE law that governs the church, the law that displaced the Ten Commandments, the law that overrules all human law, is the law of love.

If one walks in the Jesus kind of love he will never break any law that was given to curb sin.

When one walks in love, he actually walks in God, for God is love.

When one walks in love, he is no longer negative or neutral.

He is a positive element of blessing in the world.

When one steps out of the love law, he steps out of the environment of God, and into the environment of the adversary.

When one acts out of love, he acts in harmony with the adversary; he puts himself in a place where he has no defense. The adversary has the mastery.

As long as he walks in love, Satan has no dominion over him.

When one acts out of love he weakens the faith element in him.

We cannot walk by faith without walking in love.

We cannot live the faith life without living the love life.

It took me a long while to get this clear in my own spirit, but now I know it.

Our faith will unconsciously be measured by our love walk.

We cannot talk out of love nor act out of love without weakening our faith.

I Cor. 13 Love "seeketh not its own." Faith in the Father and selfishness do not mix.

When we walk by faith, we become independent of circumstances.

When we walk in love, we walk in the realm of the Father's protection and we walk in His wisdom.

The Father is love, and He is light.

He has made Jesus to be wisdom unto us.

When we walk in fellowship with Him we have wisdom; we have His ability.

Faith becomes as natural to us as water is natural to a fish.

It is a part of our being.

God is to us our strength, our life, our ability.

The Effect of Righteousness in the Presence of Disease and Sickness

We have wondered why Jesus was so utterly fearless in the presence of Satan and of his works.

We saw Him in the presence of death at Lazarus' tomb, with a fearless confidence that thrilled us.

Why was it?

It was because He was Righteous.

Sin makes cowards of men. Sin consciousness holds us in bondage.

We know we are of God and we know we have God in us. We know we are the Righteousness of God. We can stand in the presence of Satan, of his works, as fearlessly as did Jesus. (Read our Book, "Two Kinds of Righteousness")

Righteousness is really the ability of God taking possession of us.

We stand in His presence utterly fearless, because of the consciousness that we are New Creations.

We have been created by God himself, and Jesus has given to us the power of attorney to use His Name.

He said, "In my name ye shall cast out demons."

If we cast out demons, we can undo anything that Satan has done.

We can break the power of Satan anywhere he is entrenched.

We can cast down and destroy his strongholds.

We can break in upon him with a fearlessness that will mean his destruction and our victory .

We know that Satan has been conquered, that we are now masters where we have been slaves, we are strong where we have been weak.

We are identified with God; we can fearlessly take His place and act as Jesus acted when He walked the earth.

It was no meaningless sentence that dropped from the lips of the Master when He said, "Greater works than these shall ye do because I go unto the Father; and whatsoever ye shall demand in my name, that will I do, that the Father may be glorified in the Son."

That, we understand, is not prayer, not talking to the Father, but talking to demons.

We put up a fearless, solid front, and face our adversary as conquerors.

Jesus said, "Come out of him."

We say, "In the Name of your Master, come out of him. Go off into the abyss where you belong, and don't ever come back and harrass and injure this man again."

We are taking Jesus' place. We are acting in His stead.

His Righteousness that has been imparted to us gives us the ability to act in His stead and to take His place.

This is a new day in the Divine Life. This is a new order in the realm of men.

Satan reigned over the old order. Sin consciousness dominated us.

We have come to know that the New Creation is the Righteousness of God in Christ.

We know that this Righteousness is not theological or philosophical, but an actual Righteousness.

It is God changing our sin consciousness to Righteousness consciousness.

It is God who has been at work within us, building His Word into our spirit until we have become God-like in our thinking, masterful in our works.

We are no longer timid and fearful.

We stand as sons of God should stand in the presence of a defeated enemy.

In I Cor. 2:6 it speaks of the dethroned powers in the world. (Moffatt's Trans.)

We have recognized them as dethroned.

We have recognized ourselves as enthroned.

God is enthroned within us.

We are the masters of the forces of darkness that have been destroying the human race.

We are going to take our place and play the part.

The Relation of Righteousness to Faith

Faith grows out of continual fellowship with the Father.

Righteousness is the ability to stand in the Father's presence without the sense of guilt or inferiority.

It is the product of the finished work of Christ that culminates in the New Creation.

When we know that the Father recreated us, with His own nature, taking out everything that was unlovely; putting His own life and nature in its place, and when we realize that He is so satisfied with the New Creation that He can make it His home, that He comes and dwells in us, we can realize how precious, how utterly priceless we are to Him.

If He had sons and daughters with whom He could not fellowship on terms of equality, there would be no satisfaction in it; the work He wrought in Christ would be an utter failure.

We are certain that man, at the beginning, had perfect fellowship with the Father, and when he fell that fellowship was broken.

A perfect Redemption must restore that lost fellowship. It must be restored on legal grounds.

Man must know that he has a perfect right in his Father's presence.

He must lay the foundation to build a perfect love life; out of this perfect love life will grow a faith life.

Faith works by love. Faith and love are kindreds.

Love gives birth to faith and faith strengthens love.

When one knows that God has recreated him, made him a new Creation, and that New Creation is the nature of the Father imparted to him, then he knows that his normal place is in the Father's presence.

Jesus said, "I am the vine; ye are the branches." That figure compels one to know that there is perfect fellowship since the branch and the vine are one.

The branch is as Righteous as the vine, for the vine has imparted its life and Righteousness to the branch.

This builds faith into the believer. We continually affirm that we are the Righteousness of God in Christ.

We say it over and over again, until the reality of it becomes a part of our consciousness.

We are as conscious of it as we are that four and four are eight, or that a fire gives off heat, or that the sun gives light.

We know that we are what God says we are.

We do not try to be what He has made us.

We enjoy the wealth and riches of what we are in Christ.

When He says He becomes the Righteousness of him that has faith in Jesus, we know God has become our Righteousness, for we have faith in Jesus as a Savior and Lord.

We know we are Righteous.

We don't try to be Righteous, anymore than a man has to try to be a man. He may try to be a good man, but he is what nature has made him.

We are what God has made us to be—His own Righteousness.

The Spirit says through Paul that God made Jesus to be wisdom unto us.

We know Jesus is our wisdom.

When He says Jesus was made unto us sanctification, we know we are sanctified by His sanctification.

When He declares He was made unto us Redemption, we know we are Redeemed, that He is our Redemption.

Consequently, our Redemption is a reality.

By the same token He declares that He has become our Righteousness.

If He has become our Righteousness, then our standing with the Father is identical with His. This is ground for a real faith in the Son of God.

Mark 11:22 (Authorized Version) "Have the faith of God." (Revised Version) "Have faith in God." We have both.

We have God's faith reproduced in us by His living Word, by His nature that is imparted to us.

We have faith in God because it is a normal, natural thing for a child to have faith in its parent.

We have more faith in the ability of God to put us over, to heal, give ability and strength, to meet life's problems, than we have in the adversary to thwart the purpose of God in us.

In other words, we have more faith in God's ability than we have in the ability of the adversary.

We have more faith in the Father's Word than we have in the circumstances that surround us or the environment that would attempt to hold us in bondage.

God is bigger to us than any other thing in the world.

We know that greater is He that is in us than the environment or the influences that surround us.

We know that we are more than conquerors, that we have passed out of the realm of failure into the realm of success and victory.

The Effect of Sin Consciousness on Faith

Faith cannot grow in the atmosphere of condemnation.

As long as we keep ourselves in the realm of sin consciousness, our faith will be weak and ineffectual.

If we attend a church where sin is preached continually, it will develop a sin consciousness and destroy faith's vigor.

Faith, like love, demands continual confession.

If we do not continually affirm our love for those about us, love will slowly congeal, become ineffective.

There must be the continual affirmation of love.

The husband and wife who cease to affirm their love for each other, slowly but surely lose the keen fellowship with each other.

The same thing is true in faith.

We constantly affirm our confidence, our faith, and it grows.

Some Affirmations to Make

"I can do all things in Him who strengtheneth me."

"God's ability is in me."

"I have the life of God abiding in me."

"Whatsoever I ask of the Father in Jesus' Name He gives it to me."

"God's strength and God's ability abide within me."

"I have His wisdom."

"I do not have to ask for wisdom, because wisdom is mine."

"I do not have to pray for faith, because His

promises cannot be broken. No Word from God is void of Power." Luke 1:37.

"I have a standing invitation to come boldly into the throne room and sit in the presence of my Father."

"I am now a member of the divine household. God is my Father. I am His child. I am in the family."

"I am a partaker of His divine nature."

"I am constantly conscious of His indwelling presence."

"Greater is He that is in me than he that is in the world."

"I have His love life abiding in me."

These affirmations build faith, health, life and strength into the believer's life.

These affirmations are the Word, or based on the Word. They are not the affirmations of Sense Knowledge.

Chapter XVIII

MY RECEIPT

WHILE talking with an aged saint the other day, who has been afflicted with kidney trouble, I called her attention to the fact that God had laid her diseases upon Jesus. I read Isaiah 53:4 to her. "Surely He hath borne our sicknesses and carried our diseases."

She said, "Yes, that's true."

I said, "Don't you see, Mother, that Scripture is your receipt for a perfect healing? It is just as though you owed a bill that you could not pay and someone handed you a receipt in full for the bill. You looked at the receipt and knew the bill had been paid.

"You rejoiced in the fact that you were free from that debt.

"The Father wants you to know that He paid the debt. He put your diseases on Jesus, made Jesus sick with your sickness. 'For it pleased Jehovah to bruise Him. He hath made Him sick.' Isa. 53:10.

"It is unseemly for you to have the disease or to ever think about the disease. This Scripture is your receipt in full, up to date, for a perfect healing of that disease.

"According to His Word, 'By His stripes you are healed' now.

"You refuse to give place to any other thought that would contradict His Word. You refuse to take the testimony of your Senses. There is the pain in your back, but you refuse to accept that as evidence that you have not been healed.

"You say confidently, quietly, 'Father, I thank Thee

that that kidney trouble was laid on Jesus, that He was made sick with it, and that by His stripes I am healed.'

"There is not a worry, there is not a fear, because Jesus bore your disease in His body on the tree.

"When 'He was stricken, smitten of God and afflicted' it was with your diseases.

"'He was bruised for your iniquities and the chastisement of your peace was upon Him and with His stripes you are healed.' That is your receipt in full.

"You were delivered from the dominion of the adversary. You are free."

She said, "I see it."

Sin and Sickness Problems Settled

At one time I was very anxious to prove that Jesus was actually raised from the dead, that He actually ascended into heaven with His own blood and presented it in the Heavenly Holy of Holies and that Justice accepted it.

I was desperately anxious to know this was true.

If this was true, then the sin and sickness problems were settled and Satan's dominion over me was ended.

If Jesus sat down at the right hand of God, then disease has no claims upon my spirit, soul or body.

Heb. 9:11-12 (Cent. Trans.) "But when Christ came, a High Priest of good things to come, he passed through the greater and more perfect tent not made with hands, that is to say, not of this material creation, not taking the blood of goats and oxen, but his own blood, and entered once for all into the Holy Place, obtaining for us an eternal redemption."

This answered my question. He had made an Eternal Redemption for me for spirit, soul and body.

Christ bore my sicknesses and He carried my diseases, and by His stripes I was healed.

If Jesus sat down at the right hand of God, that fact is a receipt in full for the sin problem and the disease and sickness problem.

I can't tell you how feverishly I went through the Scriptures to prove this. I found that nineteen or more times it declares that "He sat down."

He sat down because He had set me free, because He had satisfied the claims of justice. He had broken the dominion of the adversary.

"He had put sin away by the sacrifice of Himself." Heb. 9:26.

He had made Righteousness available. (2 Cor. 5:21) He had made Eternal Life certain. (I John 5:13)

That means that every Word in the New Testament is backed by Jesus, Himself. Behind Jesus is the throne of God. Behind the throne is God, Himself.

I Peter 2:24 "Who his own self bare our sins in his own body on the tree." That is not only the solution of the sin problem, but of the problem of sins. The sin problem was what we were. Sins were what we had done. He put sin away and remitted our sins.

"That we might live unto Righteousness."

That we might live in the realm of Righteousness. That means that we stand in the Father's presence just as the Master, without any sense of guilt or inferiority.

We take our place as the sons and daughters of God Almighty, members of His own family, joint heirs with His own Son.

Unless we do take our place, we deny the efficacy of His Blood, and the reality of His Sacrifice and the integrity of His Redemption.

When we take our place we honor the Father. We honor the Son. We honor the New Creation in Christ Jesus.

We honor our own position. How important it is that we grasp the significance of this.

"By whose stripes ye were healed." That is the conclusion of the whole matter.

Sin is put away. Righteousness is a fact.

Disease is a thing of the past.

According to this Scripture and Paul's Revelation of Christ's finished work, we should never again be under the dominion of the adversary.

We should study to show ourselves approved unto God, Christians that need not be ashamed, taking our place in the family without condemnation.

"How will we ever die?" someone asks.

We should simply wear out and fall asleep without pain, without these hideous diseases that dishonor our Lord.

What a life, what a Redemption, what a relationship is ours!

Chapter XIX

WHAT JESUS SAID ABOUT FAITH

HY Jesus demanded Faith of the Jews bothered me at first, then I saw why. He was speaking to God's Covenant people who had broken faith with Jehovah.

Matt. 9:28-30 when the two blind men came for healing He said, "Believe ye that I am able to do this? They say unto him, Yea, Lord. Then touched he their eyes, saying, According to your faith be it done unto you. And their eyes were opened."

He said to Martha, "If thou believest" thou shouldst see the glory of God."

Again He said, "All things are possible to him that believest."

What were they to believe . . . not that He died for their sins and arose for their Justification, not that He was their Substitute who had put their sin away, not that if they accepted Him as a personal Savior and confessed Him as their Lord they would receive Eternal Life.

What kind of faith did He demand?

It was not saving faith as we understand it. "Because if thou shalt confess with thy mouth Jesus as Lord, and believe in thy heart that God raised Him from the dead, thou shalt be saved."

He never asked anyone to believe in Him as a Savior who was to give men Eternal Life.

He asked them to believe that He was the Son of God, the Healer, the Messiah.

He did not ask them to believe in what we call His Substitutionary Sacrifice.

He never mentioned it. He did not ask them to believe in His Resurrection, for He had not yet died and risen from the dead.

Mark 11:20-24 is suggestive. They saw the fig tree withered away from the roots. Peter calling to remembrance saith unto him, "Behold, the fig tree which thou cursedst is withered away. And Jesus answering saith unto them, Have faith in God."

Then He said, "For verily I say unto you, That whosoever shall say unto this mountain, Be thou removed, and be thou cast into the sea; and shall not doubt in his heart, but shall believe that those things which he saith shall come to pass; he shall have whatsoever he saith.

"Therefore I say unto you, What things soever ye desire, when ye pray, believe that ye receive them, and ye shall have them."

He is not talking to the Church. He is talking to Jews under the First Covenant, yet in a way it applies to us.

He is demanding that they believe in Him.

They can see Him as a man. They see His miracles. He has fed the multitude; He has turned water into wine; He has walked upon the sea; He has ruled the winds and the waves; He has raised the dead.

John 6:29 The Jews said to Him, "What then doest thou for a sign, that we may see and believe?"

Theirs was Sense Knowledge Faith. They believed in what they saw or heard.

John 20:24-29 is the story of Thomas' unbelief.

He said, "Except I shall see in his hands the print of the nails, and put my finger into the print of the nails, and thrust my hand into his side, I will not believe."

Eight days after that Jesus suddenly appeared to Thomas and said, "Reach hither thy finger, and behold my hands; and reach hither thy hand, and thrust it into my side; and be not faithless, but believing."

Jesus was not asking Thomas to believe that He had arisen from the dead because He had put his sin away. He was challenging his Sense Knowledge Faith to actually believe in Him.

Thomas' faith was in the Senses: what he could see, feel and hear.

You can understand that no one who walked with Jesus had faith in the sense that Paul has told us in the Book of Romans.

Jesus never demanded that anyone believe in Him as a Savior who was going to die and rise again for their Justification.

In John 11:27 Martha said to Jesus, "I have believed that thou art the Christ, the Son of God, even He that cometh into the world."

That is not a confession of salvation.

Had Martha confessed salvation from sin she would have said, "Yes, Master, I have believed thou art the Son of God. I believe you are going to die for my sins and you are going to rise again for my Justification."

John 20:9 "For as yet they knew not the Scripture, that he must rise again from the dead."

After He arose from the dead no one expressed faith in Him as the Savior from sin and the giver of Eternal Life and the Author of the New Birth.

They believed that He arose from the dead.

The Pauline Revelation had to come before this knowledge of Christ as a Substitute, and the

112

knowledge of the New Creation could be known.

Jesus said, "When He, the Spirit of Truth is come, He will guide you into all truth. He shall glorify me, for He shall take of mine and shall declare it unto you."

This indicates that there was to be a Revelation of Jesus and the Father beside what Jesus taught in His earth walk.

That Revelation came to the Apostle Paul.

The basis of it is found in the first ten chapters of Romans.

There is revealed to us a Righteousness from God to the man who believes in Jesus.

Righteousness means the ability to stand in God's presence as free from sin consciousness as Jesus was in His earth walk.

There is no hint of that in Jesus' teaching.

What Paul Taught

Israel's faith was all future.

Our faith finds its root in the past in what God did for us in Christ. Abraham looked unto the promise and never questioned or challenged it.

We look at the New Testament, the fact of our Redemption, of our healing, of the Father's care for us, and like Abraham we wax strong giving glory to God.

Here are a few simple facts that we as sons of God are to act upon.

Eph. 1:3 "Blessed be the God and Father of Our Lord Jesus Christ, who hath blessed us with every spiritual blessing in the heavenlies in Christ."

That means that the moment we accept Jesus Christ as our Savior and confess Him as our Lord,

113

everything God wrought in Christ belongs to us. It is ours.

Just as Jesus belongs today to the world because God said in John 3:16 "For God so loved the world, that He gave His only begotten Son."

God gave Jesus to the world. The unsaved man does not need to ask for Jesus as a Savior. Jesus belongs to the unsaved man.

The Father has never taken that gift back. That gift today belongs to the people for whom it was given.

When you accept that gift, everything that Jesus did for you belongs to you.

This has been hard for us to accept.

We have been taught that we must pray and agonize and cry for these things.

They are ours.

The Holy Spirit has been given to the Church.

Luke 11:13 "If ye then, being evil know how to give good gifts unto your children, how much more shall your heavenly Father give the Holy Spirit to them that ask Him?"

The moment you are Born Again, that moment He is yours for the asking.

Eternal Life belongs to the sinner.

The moment he accepts Jesus Christ, he gets Eternal Life.

"By grace are ye saved through faith, and that not of yourself; it is the gift of God."

It is a gift. "We are His workmanship created in Christ Jesus."

When were we "created in Christ Jesus?" During the three days and three nights before He arose from the dead.

When were we declared Righteous? "He was delivered up on the account of our trespasses and raised when we were Justified," (or declared Righteous) .

Righteousness is a gift. Salvation is a gift. It is not something we have to earn.

In the Revelation that God gave to Paul, He demanded that the sinner have faith in what He did in Christ for him.

The sinner must believe that Jesus died for his sins and rose again from the dead.

Paul's Revelation declares that after you have believed, the problem of faith is not raised again, for all things belong to you.

You need not exercise faith to get what is yours. It is only necessary to know they belong to you.

SUMMARY

You have read it. What are your reactions?

Much has been new to you.

Some of it has confused you because it was so different from anything you have heard before.

Your heart knows that it is true.

What are you going to do with it?

The Church is in a desperate condition.

There is little active, living faith among believers anywhere.

Won't you help us spread this glorious truth that makes the Father and Jesus, the Spirit and the Word real?

Ask your Sunday School teacher to read it to the class.

Invite a few of your friends in and read and discuss it with them.

See that your pastor and every Bible teacher in your community has a copy.

Let us hear from you!

Read our other books; they will help you.

A SUGGESTION

You have seen the difference between faith in the Senses and faith in the Word.

What is your responsibility toward those who are living in the Senses yet are struggling to get results that can only come through faith in the Word?

"But," you say, "how can I help them?" You can help them by circulating this literature, forming reading classes in your community, telling the people what God can do for them through these books.

If you haven't read the other books published by this author, be sure to get them.

You want to have a share in this great ministry, I know. If it is not convenient to organize a class, wouldn't the Lord enjoy having you sell the books?

We are depending upon those who read our literature and are helped by it to help us give it to the world.